THE SEVEN AGES OF MAN

GEORGE WILLIAM RUTLER

THE SEVEN AGES OF MAN

Meditations on the Last Words of Christ

IGNATIUS PRESS   SAN FRANCISCO

Calligraphy by Joan McGrady-Beach
Cover art by Christopher J. Pellicano

With ecclesiastical approval
© 1991 Ignatius Press, San Francisco
All rights reserved
ISBN 0-89870-361-1
Library of Congress catalogue number 90-85101
Printed in the United States of America

CONTENTS

All the world's a stage,
And all the men and women merely players:
They have their exits and their entrances;
And one man in his time plays many parts,
His acts being seven ages. At first, the infant,
Mewling and puking in the nurse's arms.
Then, the whining schoolboy, with his satchel,
And shining morning face, creeping like a snail
Unwillingly to school. And then, the lover,
Sighing like a furnace, with a woeful ballad
Made to his mistress' eyebrow. Then, a soldier,
Full of strange oaths, and bearded like the pard,
Jealous in honour, sudden and quick in quarrel,
Seeking the bubble reputation
Even in the cannon's mouth. And then, the justice,
In fair round belly, with good capon lin'd,
With eyes severe, and beard of formal cut,
Full of wise saws and modern instances;
And so he plays his part. The sixth age shifts
Into the lean and slipper'd pantaloon,
With spectacles on nose, and pouch on side;
His youthful hose well sav'd, a world too wide
For his shrunk shank; and his big manly voice,
Turning again toward childish treble, pipes
And whistles in his sound. Last scene of all,
That ends this strange eventful history,
Is second childishness, and mere oblivion;
Sans teeth, sans eyes, sans taste, sans everything.

As You Like It

CHAPTER ONE

INFANCY

"Father, forgive them, for they know not what they do."

Accomplices in Creation

To BE STILL for any length of time is a test, and what may seem to be taxed patience could just be evidence of vitality; for though the splendid fact comes to be taken for granted, we are alive. Nothing alive is fixed and unchanging. Patience would not be a virtue were it inertia, and tranquility is a spiritual good when it is not decay. There is no virtue in the stillness of a corpse; corpses are just dead. By neglect of this not unobvious fact, one novelist got attention in the world of letters, and from theologians, with his sentence: "The dead sea was alive with corpses."

As every really living thing is not only moved but moves other things and is ordered to an end however you want to define it, life is in dramatic tension. When you put that drama in ample greasepaint and seedy declamations, you get melodrama where the figure on stage cries, "Curtains!" and collapses with a satisfying thud. But in the unaffected play of ordinary existence some sort of physical curtain does indeed come down eventually; and so does a moral curtain descend, for man is soul as well as body.

As a moral fact, boredom is thirst for drama and the simple longing to be an accomplice in creation. Dramas have plots; and life, as the definitive drama, is the essential and gratuitous plot from which manufactured plans and schemes flow. God alone knows the full plot by the Creator's ability to "see" it all at once: thus God does not have the theological virtue of faith, if only because he does not

need it. He is not "theological" in any way because he is
Theos and he is Logos, and so too he who is the hope of
the world does not have the theological virtue of hope. It
does not follow from this that his world is hopeless; it does
mean that he has no hope for the world precisely because
he is its hope. The world could be hopeless only if it were
godless. Of course the world may act as though it were
godless, but this is only bad acting; its true nature consists
in its being a creation of God, and the dramatic tension
within worldliness consists in the coexistence of creatureliness and the denial of a Creator. This at least may be said:
human intelligence has some partial knowledge of what
has happened—that forms history; and because the script
continues, the human mind also envisions a future. As a
specimen is put under the microscope for examination and
analysis, representative human acts are put on stages, their
drama "stretched out" or "dramatized" for the scrutiny of
those, that is, all of us, who are temporal agents of God's
eternal design.

The worth of a play depends on its subject, but no
subject is quite worthy of attention if it does not refer,
in one or another way, to the higher principles of life,
and these in turn are "higher" than the "lower" concerns
of existence according to their connection with God. This
does not have to be self-conscious, and it is probably
best to avoid aiming at "grandeur" or else we will end up
with those pageants of vague religiosity and overreaching
attempts at portentousness based on feelings that fizzle out
when the nice weather changes or you run out of caffeine.
"Feel Good" religion is not much of a religion, and nothing calls its bluff more quickly than feeling bad. God did
not become man to make us feel good or even to improve
us; his whole purpose was to save us from sin and death so

that we might have eternal life. One of the prejudices that make this a difficult object of assent is the notion of perfection as a form of psychological conditioning, a correction of manners, and Christ censures this from the start: " . . . you clean the outside of the cup and of the plate, but inside they are full of extortion and rapacity" (Mt 23:25). Perfection is far more violent and transforming than that; it does not reshape life so much as it gives new life. How this happens without changing identity is a grand mystery, but it does happen, and the saints are there to show how it happens.

Some saints are great reformers, and some have been quite removed from the market of deeds and ideas, but the concept of spirituality without social consequence is of course idle pietism. It obtains in some religions, like Hinduism, which are older than Christianity, and indeed the Judaic social consciousness is exceptional among pre-Christian forms; but love as a social virtue becomes almost synonymous with the very concept of religion after Christ. Its application becomes aberrant in Christian spirituality principally because of the doctrine of salvation by faith alone. If there is to be any salvation, it will not be by the assent of faith alone (Martin Luther added the exclusive qualifier and so got it wrong). It will come by the fullness of faith manifest in good works, which are the effective evidence of saving grace.

At the same time there is the other, not contradictory, truth: works without faith are just monochrome busyness. Unchecked, this produces the religious fidget full of abstract responsibilities, an annoyance who blurs the line between inspiration and neurosis, seeking to do good through a dozen committees and schemes as a sublimation of personal inadequacy or untested virtue; no one is surer to convert sensible people to irreligion and to make the Christian drama a pantomime. And this is just what comes from the mental mosaic of Christ as a reformer but not a redeemer. The Bleeding Heart on the cross saves us from much, and that includes the lesser "bleeding heart" reformer who would scrub us up through some human collective action. Probably most people who make that mistake do not even realize that there is a difference, nor can it be realized without acknowledging the existence of sin. If the world is only bent out of shape you only have to bend it back, which the Red Cross can do as well as the redder cross of Christ; but if it is broken it has to be completely repaired. Reform bends, redemption replaces, and only God, who is not part of the fracture, has the leverage in eternity to fix it in time.

The descriptions of how that takes place on Calvary are various: Christ substitutes himself for fallen humanity, he sacrifices himself, he makes himself an example, and so forth. None is quite adequate of itself to describe it all, but the redemptive fact is one great drama, and any critique that does not acknowledge this is only confessing its own triviality. One conspicuous evidence of the banal is its incapacity for the commonplace: if ordinary things are dull, then drama consists in escape from reality. Banality characteristically opts for the cartoon over the miniature. Of course human dramas, by virtue of the defects of nature, affect a certain exoticism, and theater is by definition the staging of the unreal. But even in this context, the pretense magnifies rather than distorts. And the more skilled the script, the more it locates stunning props in little things. To burlesque is to magnify the conspicuous; it drags a giant onto the scene when it lacks the delicacy for greatness and becomes a spectacle when it has lost its powers of observation. Great theater is usually about ordinary things, ordinary people, and ordinary events, and its achievement lies in focusing on how ordinariness indicates order, and how order is the most spectacular of all evidences of life.

Some plays get this right and some do not; when they fail they give the impression that order is trivial. Then, as in modern existentialist themes, they wither into a theatrical and evasive pessimism, moaning about fate as though complaining were heroic; they actually suppose that if there is a plot at all, it is a plot against life. They rather boil down to deciding whether God, whatever they call him, is plotting against us. The correct answer depends first of all on recognizing how mysterious it is to have plays at all: humans are the only creatures that build stages and act on them. As the mediaeval theologian located humanity in the ability to smile, so a corollary definition might be the capacity for staging plays: this has nothing to do with the evolution of large thumbs or cranial capacity, and it has everything to do with the inspiration that can imagine an "eternal instant", for the eternal instant is what theater strives to produce. If all creatures act as living factors in the drama of existence, humans are the creatures that act within the act and rivet human experience to a flash of words. The human intellect weaves on the mental loom what are incomprehensibilities for any other creature: reflections and projections, histories and predictions, philosophies and prophecies. There is no clearer hieroglyphic of the human mystery than people watching a play, unless it is a sweaty crowd watching a sweatier man dying on a cross, as though this were the fever and all the universe the brow.

In the three hours of the Agony on the cross is a drama unlike others. It is not one of our self-consciously crafted productions. The recapitulation of the world's own biography is exposed before human eyes. Other scenes act out truths; this is the Truth in action. As the Truth becomes the one authentic man, there is nothing false in where he is. The stage is a hill, and if the imagination says it looks like a skull, the imagination is informed by solid rock. The props are not false; they are two plain pieces of wood making a cross, and the backdrop is the sky filled with a frenzy of hawks. The stark actor is one of ourselves. For Jesus was a baby as you and I once were; and he "grew up", that term so terrible in wonder that it dares sound quaint, as you and I grow up; and on the cross Jesus is dying as you and I must do. The Fathers of the Second Vatican Council described the setting lived in by the Fathers of all the other councils:

> . . . it is the world as the theatre of human history, bearing the marks of its travail, its triumphs and failures, the world which in the Christian vision has been created and is sustained by the love of its makers, which has been freed from the slavery of sin by Christ, who was crucified and rose again in order to break the stranglehold of the evil one, so that it might be fashioned anew according to God's design and brought to its fulfilment (*Gaudium et Spes,* no. 2).

In the Forest of Arden

In words almost as well known as Scripture, Shakespeare listed in soliloquy the passages of human life. *As You Like It* (II. vii. 139) has a tiresome player named Jaques, little improved for having given up his libertine ways, affected in melancholy and officially subacid, who wants to sober a feast begun in the Forest of Arden. And as becomes apparent,

INFANCY 17

he is not much welcome. When what is wanted is a song, his half-repentant psychology drops a dismal note, like a slightly manic gloss on heartier creeds and councils:

> All the world's a stage,
> And all the men and women merely players:
> They have their exits and their entrances;
> And one man in his time plays many parts,
> His acts being seven ages.

The seven last lines Jesus spoke from the cross address the seven ages of man, if only by being ageless words for the aging, and the finest speeches about those ages from the most treasured literature of the theater are nervous sketches of what God himself knows about the drama he has set in motion. The Abbé Gaume's *Catechism of Perseverance* touched on it too, more prosaically, by starting at the beginning like all good catechisms; and without such reference, human consideration of the human condition has to be either pessimistic like Jaques, or fantastic like the singers in the Forest of Arden, or both:

> From all eternity God had conceived the idea of the world. At the time marked out for it, He uttered the thought, that is, He expressed His outwardly by *His Word,* in short, He spoke, and all things were made. . . . To know how powerful and fruitful was the Word that created the universe, let us hear the account of the creation with the same sentiments of admiration penetrating our souls as if we had been present at this great work, and had seen, at each word of the Creator, the wondrous multitude of creatures, so various and so perfect, spring forth from nothingness. Before our eyes will be unfolded a magnificent book, the first in which God desires that the children of men should read the lesson of

His existence, glory, power, goodness, and all His other perfection. . . .

Each indignity and violation that Christ endured on the cross was to employ his perfection to save this creation from what had sullied its gift of life. And as creation came through divine utterance, so he utters words from the cross that can recreate his creatures. Each of his utterances, or "words", touches upon the seven human ages because in retrospect, anything human playwrights have proposed in ink and shouts about the art of living have at least occasionally, and usually very obliquely, touched on the absolute truths that Christ addressed in blood and cries. This is no more coincidental than the seven acts, or "days", of creation themselves. Each of us has had an infancy as did the universe; and Shakespeare's man, no anarchist in the regiment of chronology, starts here:

> At first the infant,
> Mewling and puking in the nurse's arms.

That is how we were; but what the soliloquy does not dare approach, and the venture would offend its agreeable melancholy if it did, is that this is also how our Redeemer God came into the world. The Word was made flesh, and it was the flesh of a baby, doing unexceptionally things a baby does. In legends there were gods who came into this world full grown by fugitive agency, like Minerva springing from the brow of Jupiter or born like Venus full-fledged of the sea foam, whole in diaphanous enchantments. That is the stuff of what never happened and the fantasy of what should have been had human imagination designed perfection. God could have done that, for he is God; but for our sake he became perfectly human.

He did not come as a triangle, presumably because we are not triangles. On the other hand, he did not come as a defective human because we are not supposed to be defective. Change is not a defect but an essence of life, so Christ comes first as a baby that grows and changes. It was the form of compliment God pays to his sons and daughters who rarely express fascination with it except perhaps for a few obligatory carols at Christmas; still, there is a shattering gallantry about the "Lord of every courtesy", as Dante called him: the Perfect Man lying on straw in a diaper, and far more surprising than an imperfect man putting on a dinner jacket for breakfast. If it seems out of place or literally outlandish, that is because the human race has been out of place so long that it has forgotten how to dress.

Eternity Confined

It would not hurt our eternal future to consider the economy of change as passionately as experts size up the changing economy, although it would traumatize our preconceptions. But since change is rampant in the definitive drama of the created dimension, any other approach is tantamount to evasion and unreality. "Growth the only evidence of life" was an axiom of the early nineteenth-century clergyman, Thomas Scott, and by its long influence John Henry Newman would come to write more: "In a higher world it is otherwise, but here below to live is to change, and to be perfect is to have changed often." Jesus grew from infancy into manhood, and on the cross he would seem in carnal terms to have been forced into a second infancy. To the eye of the Jew, that was the critical horror of the cross. The pain was one thing, and Jews

pitied that, but most appalling about this device for killing
a man was the way it reduced him to physical helplessness
and became the publicity of infantilism. The cross was a
grim machine in itself; it strained the heights of the maca-
bre when it imitated a cradle. The Romans took the method
from the Phoenicians and made it more efficient to the
astonishment of the people God had chosen to teach the
unique dignity of man. If the Jews sympathized and even
empathized with the pain, they were embarrassed by the
shame, and this took on the moral architecture of scandal.

When our Lord was taken down from the cross and
returned to the arms of his mother, he, as all the crucified
were, was covered with his own waste and tears. And this
is not to be forgotten if redemption is not to be forgotten.
Mary did not forget that as she was led from Golgotha.
She could have traveled through a mental corridor back to
Bethlehem, where the mewling and puking infant nursed
in her arms was her own Lord. Christianity may seem
positively offensive when it defies gentle legend with hard
truth, and there have been those through the ages most
offended to find the tale of Minerva the mother of gods
overshadowed by this fact of Mary the Mother of God.

Is infancy a defect in Christ? To be perfect is to have
changed often, and God who was born a baby of the
Virgin Mary for our sake and became a man for our sake
now dies perfectly without prejudice to his divinity in
what appears to be a return to the helplessness of the
newborn. "For Christ also died for sins once for all, the
righteous for the unrighteous, that he might bring us to
God, being put to death in the flesh but made alive in the
spirit . . . " (1 Pet 3:18). He had two natures, human and
divine. The human is not at the expense of the divine, and
the divine is not at the expense of the human. He grows

"in wisdom and stature, and in favor with God and man" (Lk 2:52), in human knowledge. Mary and Joseph teach him how to use his human sensory faculties and to survive in the natural order.

As a human Jesus has a past, present, and future. He can speak in the past tense: "Have I been with you so long, and yet you do not know me, Philip?" (Jn 14:9). He can say in the present tense, "Believe me that I am in the Father and the Father in me . . . " (Jn 14:11). And he is able to say in the future tense, "Whatever you ask in my name I will do it . . . " (Jn 14:13). So speaks a human nature, but the divine nature to which it is intrinsically united is changeless. Within each temporal utterance is the proclamation of the divine: "I am." No past, no future but a timeless present. Men and women may dramatize life because they are alive; Christ is the drama, for he is the life of the living. God Incarnate is the Eternal Instant who instances eternity.

But the loving knowledge with which the divine Redeemer has pursued us from the first moment of His Incarnation is such as completely to surpass all the searchings of the human mind; for by means of the beatific vision, which He enjoyed from the time when He was received into the womb of the mother of God, He has forever and continuously had present to Him all the members of His mystical Body, and embraced them with His saving love. How wonderful is the condescension of God's mercy towards us! How far beyond price His measureless love! In the manger, on the Cross, in the eternal glory of the Father, Christ sees and embraces all the members of His Church, and He sees them far more clearly, embraces them far more lovingly, than does a mother the child of her bosom, far better than a man knows and loves himself (Pius XII: *Mystici Corporis,* no. 75).

"Heaven lies about us in our infancy", says Wordsworth. It can be said of Christ, though a naturalist like Wordsworth does not venture it, that heaven lies in him in his infancy; there it never changes as his body changes, for the whole purpose of his moving closer to the cross is to make it possible for every soul to be in heaven, fulfilling the most curious and shattering of history's promises: "The kingdom of God is not coming with signs to be observed; nor will they say, 'Lo, here it is!' or 'There!' for behold, the kingdom of God is in the midst of you" (Lk 17:21).

Mary and Joseph teach him how to read the Scriptures that he has inspired their ancestors to chant in desert and synagogue. Joseph teaches him how to put pieces of wood together and not in the way that lesser men will assemble them on an eminence outside the city wall. All the while as they teach, they know he has another and true Father; and an unspoken and immeasurably different and more perfect consciousness of this is absorbed by him as well. Baby-talk and God-talk are the same in this one infant of all those who ever lived or ever will tenant the earth. There have been countless unimaginative attempts to level out this deep mystery into a flat enigma: pantheism, or ecology as theology, for instance, which makes creatures God; and angelism, or psychology as theology, which paints a surrealist picture of human creatures as sinless. But these are only the easiest of the many ways the mind can distract itself from the enormous challenge of God coming into his creation to redeem it from sin.

All heresies and superstitions follow the flight from the Word-made-flesh. Their common offence is not, as some apologists put it, making God too small; the difficulty behind these errors of belief and understanding is making God too abstract to be large or small and too contingent to

come "into" things without being absorbed by them or
absorbing them. Nonetheless, there was an Incarnation,
and the miracles and Passion and Resurrection of the Word-
made-flesh are not half the mental challenge that the Incarnation itself is. Acknowledge the Incarnation, and other
things fall into place; but without it, all the Christian
claims on belief and behavior are preposterous. When
d'Alembert could not believe the legend of Saint Denis
carrying his head a full two leagues, the Marquise du
Deffand replied: "The distance doesn't matter: it's the first
step that counts." And once you get through the first
proclamation of the Gospel, that God was in Christ reconciling all things to himself, then any corollary articles of
belief are ways of praising the proclamation; but when the
proclamation is qualified, when Christ is other than immortal Love come into his creation, then everything else that
can be said about him is the decible of poetry or lunacy. In
academic convention the polite way of toning down the
poetry and confining the lunacy is to say it is "nuanced".
Now, in the instance of Saint Denis' head it would be
lunacy itself to say otherwise, but the Gospel is not a
legend to prove a point, and it would be pointless to
dedicate oneself to such a point. True, great matters require
a "leap of faith", but a lunatic leaps differently than a
gymnast; it is a great mistake in theology, and one that
unfortunately has parted very many from Catholicism, to
portray faith as a substitute for reason when, as all the
Doctors of the Church have taught, it is reason's fulfillment.

    The ability of Christ to enjoy the Beatific Vision while
on earth then does not diminish his humanity or his significance for the fallen human condition; it does make clearer
what humanity and its purpose are. There has walked
among us One who is in this life the whole drama at once,

not having to pass through states of perfection. We do, of course, have to develop through these states; and as Aquinas typically specifies them they are clear and distinct. As natural persons, we reflect creation (*imago creationis*); when in the state of grace we reflect God's renewed creation (*imago recreationis*); and in heaven we would reflect God himself (*imago similitudinis*). Faith assents to the truth of this One who from the start in his human nature possessed what for us would be the final perfection (cf. S Th. I.2ae. q.93, a.4,c).

The drama of living, as it affects the life of the mind, requires that we perceive the drama of truths that, without supernatural agency, would indeed be the most extravagant self-contradictions. And nowhere is this clearer, and more offensive to limited perception, than in the infancy of the Eternal Word. The Incarnation turned the hair of history white. Let humility simply admit that what he sees when he looks "closely" is beyond human categorization. As the adults waft the flies from him in the manger, he can see the invisible angels of heaven; and if the eyes of cattle give the infant fright, he can see in them the globe of universality itself silently shining. "For in him all the fullness of God was pleased to dwell, and through him to reconcile to himself all things, whether on earth or in heaven, making peace by the blood of his cross" (Col 1:19–20). "Cradle to grave" security is an illusion without the cracks of crosses. Sane souls, the sanest, have learned and taught this: comforting assurance of life lived without confessing the redemptive power of suffering is cradle to grave insecurity. Christ shook the rafters of chronology and perception to proclaim this, and he lived it by the sheer fact of his radical obedience to the will of his Father, in his infancy and in his manhood. The Apostle learned it until he became it:

For many, of whom I tell you even with tears, live as
enemies of the cross of Christ. Their end is destruction,
their god is the belly, and they glory in their shame, with
minds set on earthly things. But our commonwealth is
in heaven, and from it we await a Savior, the Lord Jesus
Christ, who will change our lowly body to be like his
glorious body, by the power which enables him even to
subject all things to himself (Phil 3:18–21).

More Than Tragedy

Once near the beginning of his life's work, John Henry
Newman asked his congregation to indulge what tested his
characteristic delicacy of expression; then he proceeded to
preach (and this was over one hundred and fifty years
ago):

> What if wicked men took and crucified a young child?
> What if they deliberately seized its poor little frame, and
> stretched out its arms, nailed them to a cross bar of
> wood, drove a stake through its two feet, and fastened
> them to a beam, and so left it to die? It *is* almost too
> shocking . . . and ought not to be said (*Parochial and
> Plain Sermons,* VII, Sermon 10).

What if? The Man on the cross was as innocent as when he
was a baby, more innocent than the most helpless baby still
lying in its mother's womb. Now for Newman's congregation and for us comes the huge question: "Why are you
shocked at the crucifixion of a baby, and why are you not
shocked at the crucifixion of Christ?" Our Lord was on
the cross three hours, and in the same space of time in any
large American city hundreds of unborn babies are being
crucified. They are not being "terminated" for if they are
not brought to term below they will be brought to term

above. All life is according to the Creator's terms, and to kill innocent life against those terms is to nail that life through and through with another's selfish will. Not as many people are shocked at that as should be, and not many are shocked at what is happening on the cross of Christ. If all the agony of the world, if all the plagues of the world, if all the deathbed sufferings and feverish tossings, if all the unjust wars and unhealed wounds, if all the open sores were pressed into one long scream it would not be so unbearable as what is cried now from the cross.

Yet none of this is tragedy. In tragic drama the characters are victims of fate. Christ is a victim of providence. He planned it. This is the Lamb that was slain "before the foundation of the world" (Rev 3:8). He was to be born in his innocence to die for souls in their guilt. When light comes again to his risen face, he will say: "O foolish men, and slow of heart to believe all that the prophets have spoken! Was it not necessary that the Christ should suffer and enter into his glory?" (Lk 24:25–26). To suffer, he seeks a cruel age in which to be born and a land too hard to lay his head. He came into a time of sharp knives. At the dedication of the Flavian amphitheater in Rome, five thousand animals were slaughtered as public entertainment, and we are told that the lives of some slaves were so desperate that they willingly thrust their heads into the spokes of onrushing chariot wheels to end the misery.

The king under whom Jesus was born was ruthless on a scale that only modernity has learned to surpass. Whatever threatened him, or threatened to threaten him, he would destroy. His wife and mother-in-law died for their vexatious plotting; so too did the deadly wrath snuff out his sons Alexander, Aristobulus, and Antipater. He ordered the killing of children in the small town of Bethlehem to cancel the rumor of a king born there. He who gouged lands and received from Augustus the rights to half the tin mined in Cyprus could afford to indulge those who did not threaten him: once he went the length of donating some of his gold furniture for famine relief. Without justice, love wastes away into sentimentalism, and sentimentalism exhausts definition except as the attempt to love without sacrifice. On one recent occasion when hundreds of thousands of "pro-choice" demonstrators marched through the glaring alabaster city of Washington demanding permission to kill unborn babies, one contingent wore white dresses as a uniform, like the living elders before the Throne of the Lamb that was Slain; but they had no intention of self-sacrifice nor was any justice in their chants, "crucifying again to themselves the Son of God, and making him a mockery" (Heb 6:6). A sea of euphemisms is not quantity enough to purge the fatal consequence and physical agony of love tortured and turned inside out.

Triumph over Sentiment

Monstrous affection of philanthropy exacts the sacrifice of others by its own vacuousness. The ego becomes a hole that "fulfills" itself by devouring other selves, leaving behind a trail of castaway dignity like remnant bones on a beach. Gathered at the foot of the cross as actors whose scripts have been authored by the intuitions and habits of lifetimes, the lawyers in magisterial robes are sentimentally cruel, and the interpreters of the law in consecrated tassels are sentimentally cruel, and the enforcers of the law in metal plate are sentimentally cruel. "But to what shall I compare this generation? It is like children sitting in the market places and calling to their playmates, 'We piped to you and

you did not dance; we wailed and you did not mourn'"
(Mt 11:16–17).

In legend the goddess Athena played the first flute, but
tossed it down in disgust when she saw how puffing
disfigured her cheeks. In the mystery of the Incarnation,
our Lord takes up a flute, the moral fact of the Creator's
appeal to his creation, and plays on the instrument of his
own life and his revelations of truth a sound that "does not
restrain the lightnings" (Job 37:4). While in legend the
goddess was offended by how puffing the song distorted
her material form, the Christ of history is detached from
such concern precisely by his singular harmony with the
will of his Father in Heaven. To play his tune he submits to
the demands and constraints of nature, subjecting himself
to time and space, to age and decay.

> As many were astonished at him—
>   his appearance was so marred,
>   beyond human semblance,
>   and his form beyond that of the
>   sons of men—
> so shall he startle many nations;
>   kings shall shut their mouths
>   because of him;
> for that which has not been told
>   them they shall see,
>   and that which they have not
>   heard they shall understand.
>   (Is 52:14–15)

A cross cannot stop this appeal nor can crucifixion
twist it to noise. Jesus Christ was not crucified for being
ignorant of what was in the hearts of his crucifiers. He
knew their thoughts better than they knew themselves;
and his crime was to have laughed when the humans

laughed and to have cried when the humans cried. When his laughter rang out across the Galilean waves, the Devil frowned, and when he wept for Lazarus, the Devil smirked. The Evil One plays his own tunes, but he wails when worldlings laugh and laughs when they cry. On Good Friday he seeks revenge for the holy merriment that God's only-begotten Son brought to earth from heaven.

At the foot of the cross an evil vivid as electricity laughs through a crowd of mouths: "If you are the Son of God, come down from the cross!" (Mt 27:40). Jesus remains. So the Mocker turns to the men and women of this age endowed with more intelligence than judgment: "Come down from the cross! Give me your intellect!" And we do: we do each time we call truths lies and lies truths. "Come down from the cross! Give me your will" And we do: we do each time we say yes instead of no and no instead of yes. Then once we have succumbed to the mawkish modern cult of guiltless humanity, he says, "One more thing. Now that you have given me your soul, give me your babies." Then falls a deep shade over the shine that appeared when life was conceived.

Ignorance is a problem of adults. Infants know all they need to know to be infants; adults do not uniformly know how to be adults. With words of the *In Memoriam* Tennyson took note:

> The baby new to earth and sky,
>   What time his tender palm is prest
>   Against the circle of the breast,
> Has never thought that "this is I."

Adults can think "this is I", but unless they also understand themselves as creatures of the divine Other, they may be left to a life of frustration like those who deserted the scene of the crucifixion beating their breasts, less able to be themselves than babies are.

He who had been an infant nursed by another becomes a victim of the world's immaturity. And when the world of light suddenly made prosaic, having ignorantly sacrificed its own innocent young finally sacrifices the divine Innocence, he makes a higher appeal, whose full meaning will elude the intelligences of this world until the day when the secrets of all hearts are revealed: "Father, forgive them, for they know not what they do" (Lk 23:34).

CHAPTER TWO

SCHOOL

"Truly, I say to you, today you will be with me in Paradise."

The Truth Approached

AMONG THE FIRST THINGS the schoolchild learns, if not by outright indoctrination to begin with, then by playground erudition, is that there are two sides to almost everything. He has to choose sides even at play. And as years widen the frame of reference the Law of the Two Sides, if you want to call it that, a law sometimes physical and sometimes moral, becomes pervasive.

For one commonplace example, there are two sides to a coin, and our Lord knew that. He asked for a coin and said, after a kind of third-and-a-half dimensional glance, "Render to Caesar the things that are Caesar's, and to God the things that are God's." Money burns its own brand on the brain, and all three of the Synoptics record that elegant riposte (cf. Mk 12:17; Mt 22:21; Lk 20:25).

There are two sides to a street, and our Lord knew that: he preached in lanes and carriage ways and alleys. When he preached a hard saying in one of them, and by hard we mean a graphic one about eating his flesh and drinking his blood, a crew of dilettantish listeners scurried away along one side as he turned to his own men opposite: "Will you also go away?" (Jn 6:67).

There are two sides to a ship, and Jesus the carpenter knew about that. If he was not a boat builder, he was a builder of fishermen. As day was breaking on a world that seemed to these men unstrung and undone, the voice of Christ Risen called to them from the beach: "Cast the net on the right side of the boat and you will find some" (Jn 21:6). And for those who may be under an impression that this was a vague tale or literary metaphor, Saint John years later remembered the size of the fish, and that there were a hundred and fifty three of them, and the net was not torn; they were cooked on a charcoal fire and were eaten. Not to put too fine a point on it again, you have to admit that in fantasies there would be some sort of panegyric at this point, but the Fourth Gospel is content to describe ever so briefly a breakfast with a man recently dead; and so all you have is the intimation of a cluster of rough men wiping their mouths after a nervous meal on the shore of a polished sea.

So too there are two sides to conscience, and he who "perceived the thoughts of their hearts" (Lk 9:47) with a knowledge that should break guilty hearts were it not meant to stir them, knew that. A special sort of "Doppler effect" is at work with Christ, and the farther you are from him the more languidly edifying his teaching seems. The closer you get the less it seems like teaching at all and becomes a staggering and almost convulsive frequency, not the beguilement of a religious genius in any received sense, and very much like a screaming assault and a sustaining food at the same time. He makes his own living words seeds, some falling by the wayside where they are devoured by birds or fail to take real root or are choked by thorns; or else they do take real root in the intellect and will, the "good soil" of the formed conscience where they grow up and increase and yield "thirtyfold and sixtyfold and a hundredfold" (Mk 4:8).

But there is something else, and if there is not this then there is nothing, and nature itself is unfit for this world or any other: there are two sides to life. Only when I am at once bewildered and inspired by this can I claim a share in the collective conscience of moral history:

Then the King will say to those at his right hand, "Come, O blessed of my Father, inherit the kingdom prepared for you from the foundation of the world; for I was hungry and you gave me food, I was thirsty and you gave me drink, I was a stranger and you welcomed me, I was naked and you clothed me, I was sick and you visited me, I was in prison and you came to me." Then the righteous will answer him, "Lord, when did we see thee hungry and feed thee, or thirsty and give thee drink? And when did we see thee a stranger and welcome thee, or naked and clothe thee? And when did we see thee sick or in prison and visit thee?" And the King will answer them, "Truly, I say to you, as you did it to one of the least of these my brethren, you did it to me." Then he will say to those at his left hand, "Depart from me, you cursed, into the eternal fire prepared for the devil and his angels. . . ." And they will go away into eternal punishment, but the righteous into eternal life (Mt 25:34–46).

Having gone this far in acknowledging the embroidery of dualities, the balance breaks, and in fact falls into the heresy known as Dualism, if one supposes that there are two sides to the person of Christ. This concerns a distinction that eludes the literalist, like the difference between evenhandedness and ambidexterity or perspicacity and two-facedness. What makes Christ historic belongs to a dimension deeper than the dimension of historical space. He has two natures, human and divine, understanding that a nature is an essence of being; but he has only one incommunicable being, the person, which cannot be assumed but to which his human nature is assumed, and that person is divine. In the human order there are different sides to personality according to the degree of its defectiveness, and the evidence of this is the human struggle to discover its identity through various crises of life; but the divine personality of Christ, being perfect, is irreducible, and so his suffering consists in reconciling human fragmentation to his utter holiness. Caiaphas, high priest in the year of the crucifixion, "prophesied that Jesus should die for the nation, and not for the nation only, but to gather into one the children of God who are scattered abroad" (Jn 11:51–52). While charismatic leaders come and go, bringing occasional political unity, and while mellifluous teachers come and go bringing occasional philosophical agreement, Christ comes and abides in his Holy Spirit, uniting the essential identity of creatures to himself and not to a system or school.

There are no two sides to this Source of perfect integration. He is the God-Man. He is not the "Man-God" if that means he had been adopted by God at some stage in his earthly career, for Christ existed before all time as God united with his Father in the mystery of the Holy Trinity. And his return to the divine realm was an ascension in glory and not an apotheosis from manhood to divinity, like the lamentable line of self-promoters and pipers whose systems have led whole populations over cliffs in the gamut of gullible ages. Nor is he but a man who vainly thinks he is God for then he would be deluded. Nor is he God pretending to be man for that would be false and God is Truth.

There are no two sides to the living Truth. Physically there are not two Christs, and morally there are then only two ways of looking at the one true Christ. The indivisible Christ crucified is perceived morally from two sides: he is flanked by thieves, each with his own angle on the man in the middle. The one glances in pain and sees another's blood like his own, the other stares through pain and sees the blood of sacrifice. The one sees the obscene agony, and the other sees the agony of Love. The one sees the hell of a cross like his own, and the other sees by an incomplete intuition a different cross conquering hell. The one taunts as a distracting anesthetic forging each word from torture and hurling it as a hot bolt: "Are you not the Christ? Save yourself and us!" From the other side he is stopped: "Do you not fear God, since you are under the same sentence of condemnation? And we indeed justly; for we are receiving the due reward of our deeds; but this man has done nothing wrong" (Lk 23:39–41).

Reason and faith cooperate in these lines painfully spoken by the Good Thief, and were they always to work together they would resolve the conflict within each mortal soul, for they are a decision warranted by the historical adventure that claims the whole human race. We are receiving the due reward of our deeds whatever those deeds may be; the saint does not deserve honor any more than the sinner deserves forgiveness. Whatever happens to us is grace blatant though silent, the grace of justice when there is suffering and the grace of mercy when the suffering is transformed.

The Uniqueness of the Teacher

There is such a thing as justice, after all, and there is mercy. They speak from the Truth crucified in the middle of opinions: "Truly, I say to you, today you will be with me in Paradise" (Lk 23:43). Jesus is the teacher of the human race, the author of creation explaining his work. Analogies have to end here, because he is not a teacher like any other teacher. Christ is crucified, and not a similitude. He is not like anyone else, an improvement in his deportment has not made him what he is, nor is he a superior teacher through gradual access to arcane information inaccessible to dormant minds. His teaching is of a totally other order; for while teachers according to the human order pass on teachings, he passes on himself.

Take, for example, one man who had much to say about methods of teaching at the dawn of the nineteenth century. Jeremy Bentham was a Utilitarian, judging the good according to its efficiency. But there was a catch: he determined what the effect was supposed to be. "The greatest happiness of the greatest number" he called it, popularizing and politicizing a phrase of Priestley. And that number invariably came down to himself. He could not have spoken as did the Good Thief; from his economy in what he grandly set forth as *Principles of Morals and Legislation,* "All punishment is mischief: all punishment in itself is evil." He founded University College in London on what from his modest height seemed high principles, and being desirous that he preside in perpetuity over that institution he stipulated that his skeletal remains be waxed and dressed to preside over the meetings of the board of governors in perpetuity. When the board convenes, as it has ever since his death in 1832, the doors on a cabinet are open and what is left of him keeps a vacant eye on the proceedings.

That is not how Jesus Christ presides over his Church. By a great and unanticipated mystery, to which many councils have tried to reconcile the human intellect, Christ presides over the Church by residing within it. "For where two or three are gathered in my name, there am I in the midst of them" (Mt 18:20–21). The Church is his Body, and in a world whose central rule of etiquette is gradual fragmentation, or entropy, the Church is the one reality that keeps growing. And this is so, independent of numerical size or political strength up or down, for the Church grows in depth, deepening the contact of Truth with the future as it becomes present in history. It could not be otherwise, as Christ is the Beginning and the End; he has been called the Eternal Now, but he is equally the Never Past. The entire point is lost, then, if you think that the Eucharist, the central Christ act, is only a memorial like the pagan Roman *refrigerium;* or if you expect to find in the Tabernacle of a church what you find when you open the cabinet of the Governors' Room in a London university.

In the Upper Room where he gathered his men on the night before he died he took wine: "This cup which is poured out for you is the new convenant in my blood" (Lk 22:20). You can read the Bible, and you can learn from it that way; but you can only learn the Bible by drinking it. There are those who would study the Bible only as literature. Of course it is literature, but it is written in the blood of Christ. That is why it is alive. No text has been printed so indelibly or illuminated so brightly.

Even in the most material purview the vitality of Christ is astonishing. To open a copy of Plutarch's *Parallel Lives* is to see names far more noted than the obscure name of Jesus at the time of his crucifixion, names like Sethegus and Vatinius and Marcus Atho. Their celebrity means little now, like the larger number of film stars and novelists whose names have hung on the erasable slates of marquees and headlines. Scribblers no longer amuse themselves with the elegies of Propertius who was quite the rage when the three men on the cross held their fleeting conversation. As the cross of Christ intimated itself in a remote corner of the world's stage, Artabanus glistened enthroned in

Persian splendor; Arminius led flapping banners in northern Germany; from a forbidden Chinese palace Kwang Wu Ti was sending ambassadors to find a worthy god of India in which he might believe. Their shops have emptied and their names linger as curiosities of chronology. Yet when teaching in the temple precincts one Jerusalem day, the man who now is on the middle cross chose to say to people too busy to pay much attention: "Truly I say to you, this generation will not pass away till all has taken place. Heaven and earth will pass away, but my words will not pass away" (Lk 21:32–33).

Macaulay overreached himself in his essay on Lord Clive: "Every schoolboy knows who imprisoned Montezuma and who strangled Atahualpa"; but, even so, one may expect in even this late hour that there still are a great many schoolboys who know if by rumor who condemned Jesus of Nazareth. And for that matter, anyone who recites the Creed is made to repeat his name. What they may not know is that before he did it he asked this Jesus, "What is truth?" (Jn 18:38) and did not wait for an answer.

The Commitment to Objectivity

The world is still a stage and of the acts that come and go, the second act now comes into play:

> Then, the whining schoolboy, with his satchel,
> And shining morning face, creeping like a snail
> Unwillingly to school.

So far as that scene goes, it is the same as the school days of Shakespeare, except for one aneurysm that has paralyzed the life of the mind in our day, a convulsion imperceptible along the way so that it is hard to locate in any one philosopher. When the whining schoolboy went to his old school he was told to prepare for the truth. At times he was told lies as truth, or remnant and half-remembered truths, and awkward propositions as truth. At least he was told there is such a thing as truth.

Magisterial authorities in our classrooms tell shining faces that there are two sides to truth, your truth and my truth. Modern tyrannies over the mind have betrayed childhood by robbing it of a sense of the interior life of the soul, making it unfit for confidence in the truth that is Christ. In the terminology of the Angelic Doctor, *curiositas* has been substituted for *studiositas;* a concupiscence of the intellect that appropriates information for private ends has obliterated submission of the intellect to the truth for truth's sake. Truth has become subject to the disordered self that formerly at least tried to subject itself to ordered truth. The God-Man crucified between opinions about him has been made into an opinion among opinions, as though the denial of Christ is as valid as the Christ denied.

But Christ is one Divine Person even when there are different ways of looking at him. Curiosity may disagree with that, but reality shows it is so. Pride looks at him one way with eyes calcified as humility casts a vision clear. Avarice squints at him as generosity stares openly. Lust glazes over as purity gleams his way. Anger darts at him as patience studies all his form. Gluttony gapes at his sweat as temperance reflects his own shine. Envy menaces him as selflessness weeps for him. Sloth falls asleep as zeal pierces through to his very heart. But if no eye looks at him any way, no one will even know that Truth is looking out with eyes of his own.

Saint Thomas More wrote in his precocious years his

own version of the ages of man, not his best known
achievement and possibly more conventionally diagrammed
than what he would have ventured at the glorious end of
his own life. His chart of ages had four stages to which
were added, for the sake of literature and nature's grace,
the moral facts of death and fame and eternity. There was a
schoolboy in his account, too. He gets up late for school
and is frightened to go and meet the master. His mother
bids him dress, assuring him that there is precious little to
fear and sends him off. When the lad attains the entrance
to the school, reality proffers no consolation save reality
itself, and the master beats him for being late. The saint's
point is this: we can receive any number of encouraging
bromides along the way, but the truth will out in the end.

Holy Church is the world's true Mother and she never
lies, however easily the modest lie will grease the slide. She
defies the Utilitarian's Promethean contempt for childhood.
She will love her children though she knows that each is
both a sacrament of holy poverty and an incarnation of
holy terror. She will not tell us that truths are whatever
opinion elects them to be; she refuses to say the flesh is
beautified merely by being gratified; and she is incapable
of equating goodness with convenience. She is so true a
mother that she is a stern mother, and her love never
imposes itself at the expense of justice: what is right is
right and what is true is true and her peremptory warnings
are meant to save and not condemn. There is mercy in this
holy Mother, and it runs to those who fail only when they
succeed in confessing how they have failed, either through
some splendid dose of wisdom or by the hard knocks of
experience. This Mother forgives because there is something to forgive, and she saves from punishment those
souls who acknowledge the warrant for being punished.

Readers of Agatha Christie's detective books also may have read her autobiography in which she recalled a conversation with her young daughter about schools. Having visited some, the choice settled between one run by two fair but stern maiden ladies, peremptory in their rule and unbending in their schedule, and a progressive institution, freewheeling enough to allow pets and even ponies, with voluntary participation in exercises. The child offered a verdict: "Oh, Caledonia, every time. I shouldn't like the other; it would be too much like being at a party. One doesn't want being at a school to be like being at a party, does one?" She was in fact a very delightful little girl, not prim at all, and quite right. Parts of school may be like parties, but when school itself is only a party it educates in illusion. Our Lord did attend parties, to the scandal of those who probably would have dampened any one they attended, but he never promised to make life on earth a party; he promised a high feast in paradise beside which our entertainments are tinsel pastimes, and with the promise a cross as the vehicle for traveling the span between fun and joy, between pastimes and eternity, between beguilements and truth.

These things were easier for him, and his Holy Church in consequence, to explain to children than to grownups. He thus remained an inexplicable annoyance and even an object of scorn to those, like the angry thief, who thought the party was over when they looked at him. But for anyone who saw him from the proper perspective, elevated by one's cross rather than crushed by it, he was a wholly different thing, someone who could make reality heavenly and heaven real.

Disbelief and Social Penalties

At the end of the seventeenth century and beginning of
the eighteenth, the philosopher Giambattista Vico saw the
human condition in terms of God who started it going,
and as such he stood against the approaching Utilitarian
idea that founded morals and legislation merely on the
greatest happiness of the greatest number. Vico believed
that this limited functionalism would lead to a barbarism
of the spirit, regardless of external sophistication. We move,
he said, from barbarism to civilization and then into
hypercivilization, where the masses are so civilized they
can hardly bear it. And so he describes the heightened
dissolution of our time, which effects its cruelty with
stainless steel instead of stone, by neon light instead of
flickering candles, broadcasting its vain boasts on television instead of trumpets. That is where we are now. Then
must come neobarbarism, a barbarism that can reflect its
own horror, worse then the barbarism of ignorance:

> Such peoples, like so many beasts, have fallen into the
> custom of each man thinking only of his own private
> interests and have reached the extreme of delicacy, or
> better of pride, in which they bristle and lash out at the
> slightest displeasure. Thus no matter how great the throng
> and press of their bodies, they live like wild beasts in a
> deep solitude of spirit and will, scarcely any two being
> able to agree since each follows his own pleasure or
> caprice.... They shall turn their cities into forests and
> the forests into dens and lairs of men. In this way,
> through long centuries of barbarism, rust will consume
> the misbegotten subtleties of malicious wits that have
> turned them into beasts made more inhuman by the
> barbarism of reflection... (*The New Science* [Ithaca,
> NY:1968, p. 424]).

The thief goading divine Truth was a ragged end of God's faithful remnant, the son of a promise that seemed to have worn threadbare. The Jews had found their way to Jerusalem by way of a covenant, but assertions of autonomy began to disorient the homeland. The clash between the chanted Torah of the Jews and the rattling fasces of Rome had become the cacophonous barbarism of reflection attendant upon any loss of moral balance. The mocking thief on his own cross hung as a scarecrow emblem of the blindness that swears by the gold of the temple rather than by the temple, which strains at a gnat and swallows a camel, which drinks elegantly of extortion and rapacity, which adorns tombs and strips the living prophets. If this judgment is harsh, it is the judgment of God's own Son (cf. Mt 23:16ff.).

The neobarbarism was universal, as Cicero attested. In Rome the priests of the venerable Latinized pantheon made hollow prayer in their gilded Corinthian temples to gods they sensed were false, and winked when they greeted one another in the Forum. For diversion they imported cults of Isis and Astarte, diverted by the exotic as jaded moderns collect jade Buddhas and magic crystals.

So the mockery of the one thief who sees Christ one way sets the tone for every civilization bored with its own enticements, and he walks the alleys and avenues of any high-tech metropolis where drug needles litter unbreakable pavements and canned noise is amplified as the substitute for symphonies and breathtaking ignorance is handed diplomas by the world's most expensive schools. When cities become lairs, scientists in white lab coats shake their heads at incurable plagues run rampant in the glare of florescent debauchery, sociologists poke at social systems, unable to identify the purpose of society beyond pragmatic survival, inventors unveil machines making life easier for those who find it hard to understand why they are alive, and deadened judges decree that forms of life are not alive at all.

Back to School

When hypercivilization stares at its own quivering soul and sees a vacuum, it is time to go back to a real school. Blessed Edith Stein wrote of how at the age of six she had resolved to put an end to kindergarten existence and move on to the "big school". This was the only birthday present she wanted. After this subtle philosopher became a Carmelite nun, she received a horribly accurate gift when the Nazi S.S. caught her in the convent at Echt. Her school was Auschwitz where she died singing in final perfection the psalms taught her by a long civilization of the soul.

In society today more than a ripple of new confidence is stirring against the dismal surrender of the human spirit to fads and obscurantism and easy opinion. Voices in lands long oppressed are beginning to sound to a placid Western society like the Good Thief facing down the mockers of objective truth: "Do you not fear God, since you are under the same sentence of condemnation? And we indeed justly; for we are receiving the due reward of our deeds; but this man has done nothing wrong" (Lk 23:40–41). Sometimes, through the awkward and unwitting courtesy of the mass media, we receive electronic icons of how this is being played out. Take one example. Each year there is a ritual debate over who is the Man of the Year, or the Man of the Decade, or the Man of the Century. An unknown figure, little older than a school boy, has not been mentioned, but he will remain as good a candidate as any, standing in Beijing without a name, doing what no logical combatant would do. He was seen on television screens around the world, and in the United States he appeared on a news bulletin interrupting a documentary that was praising what it called the advances being made in the social fabric of China. This renegade student stretched out his arms, and for one brief moment the tank stopped. When he had been growing up, crucifixes were being removed gratuitously from classrooms in the Western world with an affected sigh of indifference. Sometimes it was done in exchange for government subsidies, like the man named Iscariot who had been the first in the history of the Church to accept a government grant. Though the student in China had not been permitted to hear of the Passion, an intuition of a higher civilization made him a living crucifix. "Jesus, remember me when you come into your kingly power" (Lk 23:42).

In a prototype of contests between power and impotence, after David had gone out with his slingshot against the champion of the Philistines and left Goliath dead, he was summoned before Saul who asked him, "Whose son are you, young man?" Whose son was the young man standing before the armored men of China, and whose sons have stocked the generations doing bold deeds? Whose son was born two thousand years ago in the City of David according to the prophets and looked to heaven as though homesick? That is the question whose answer solves the other questions, and it was the last question the two thieves had to consider as they were dying. Each approached it from a different angle, as we know, and each resolved it a different way.

It is not presumptuous to say of a truth that it is the only valid answer to a question, and the Good Thief was willing, be his muse sheer desperation, to acknowledge what the grievously wounded pride of the other man would not. Both had been boys on their way to school, whining and shining of face; and only as they were pulled up on their crosses was it evident that affliction itself was the school, and this last moment was their test. God does not expect human creatures to get all the answers right, and in the final analysis he does not ask for answers the way teachers do. From his own cross Christ only requires that the human soul ask him for the right answer, that which he has come into time to give. And to make that function as fact, the intellect will have to move from curiosity about the truth to union with it.

Prizes at commencement ceremonies, academic honors, and recognition of long accomplishments are quaint compared to the briefest of lines that he has to give in reply. When it is uttered, the futile thinness of silverplate and parchment and applause becomes evident, painfully to the proud and sublimely for those humble enough to ask for something more. That was so on the hill of Calvary and it has no capacity to cease being so. One man was never more blessed than when he heard from the very bloodied and patient Rabbi: "Truly, I say to you, today you will be with me in Paradise" (Lk 23:43). And through the Good Thief shuddering on his cross comes a benediction for the wide-roaming human race, though the crowd below called his Teacher a fraud and a liar.

CHAPTER THREE

THE LOVER

"Woman, behold your son!" . . . *"Behold your mother!"*

The World Turned Upside Down

When the Apostle Paul and his companion Silas arrived in Thessalonica of Macedonia, there was a riot of sorts. Rabble-rousers or demagogues or well-intentioned reactionaries, whatever the accusers were, said these two men had turned the world upside down and now had come to do it in their town also (cf. Acts 17). It would have been very odd, of course, to have upset the world without including Thessalonica, but this apparently had not occurred to the complainers; such is the eccentricity of jealous calculation.

The Thessalonians were mistaken: the whole world had been upside down ever since the Fall of Man, and these two men on the scene, Paul and Silas, had come to say that Jesus Christ had put it right side up again. One cannot blame the crowd for not seeing it that way; you cannot see straight when you are accustomed to living upside down. The simple fact of perspective obtains in all the disciplines and arts. When restorers cleaned the Sistine Chapel they were criticized by some experts who preferred it dirty. A glum American professor of art complained that the new appearance contradicted his theory of why Michelangelo had made the figures dark. The untrained eye of the man in the street sees dirt, and the refined eye of the man in the gallery calls it patina; but the man in the street is right. Grime is grime no matter how expensive it is. When imperfection is the rule, perfection will be an aberration. When down is thought up, any upright man will be charged with anarchy.

Things can seem an awful mess when they are precisely as they should be; perfection looks perfectly dreadful through a backwards lense. The deepest objection to heaven from those alive on earth has been that it is heavenly. And philosophers have impeached God for his holiness: the utterly Other, they have said on occasion, must be utterly Nothing. Our Lady was simply perfect, immaculately conceived, and for that reason it has been hard for many to believe she was not bizarre, or even existed. Christ was a perfect man, and so the limited human imagination easily thinks he was not human. A life so vital that it contradicted death and rose again to life was thought a threat to life: "Tell people, 'His disciples came by night and stole him away while we were asleep.' And if this comes to the governor's ears, we will satisfy him and keep you out of trouble" (Mk 28:13–14).

Instead of acknowledging the mystery of perfection, it was more plausible in the early centuries after the Passion to adapt mythological adjustments to a defective world: the various Gnostic cults, for instance, claimed a secret wisdom that could manipulate an inherently malign and suspect creation. That is far more convenient than accepting the blatant Christian paradox of original sin and Divine Providence. But paradoxes are not valid if they are not paradoxical; and once limited logic takes the contradiction out of a paradox, it is left with an agreeable lie. This is a cheap commodity for opinion, but expensive for fact. Exploring the defective shortcut of such artificial plausibilities, or "false doctrines" to use a worthy if unfashionable term, risks costly mistakes about the body, the soul, and God.

The first mistake, the one about the body, is impurity. Christ blesses the pure in heart; that is, those who have a clear vision of God for their motivation (Mt 5:8). Without that divine animating principle, purity becomes a retentive little puritanism, whether in the fiery seventeenth-century form of the Plymouth Separatists or the vegetarian twentieth-century form of the Fabian Socialists and their pallid philosophical descendants. Nothing could be more piously alien to the orthodox confidence in the original goodness of creation. For having done the will of God purely for love of God, the body and soul will be raised in holiness as part of the Creator's plan. But the Gnostic denies the providential economy of grace altogether; and this habit persists among updated modern Gnostics who claim to "celebrate life" and "affirm the self" when they introduce a sparkling neurosis as a substitute for the mystery of sin and redemption.

Gnosticism is a fluent form of pessimism, and it is never more so than when delirious with progressivist optimism contrived as a faintly compulsive substitute for the virtue of hope. Whatever ethical energies and humane sympathies may inspire the drive for utopia, at the root is abandoned hope in sanctifying grace. Of the two goriest attempts at modern utopias, one was planned by an ex-seminarian, and the other by a man who wanted his secret police to be run like the Society of Jesus without Jesus. With a dour glance, the Gnostic counsels to conquer or be conquered, and from that mental cornucopia pour a pile of blueprints for subjugating the body to mythical autonomy, the massively imprudent exaltation of the pagan state, and the graphic horrors of biological engineering and birth "control". Greed is good. Lust is good. The mind is a kingdom of its own and the body is a separate domain, morally indifferent, and you can do what you want with both.

When the Gnostic mutilation of reality appropriates religion, it promotes the Incarnation as abstraction, with Christ as some sort of aboriginal Christ figure. The Gnostic is perplexed, and not consoled, by a Christ who is not a ghost; for the entire imbalance of Gnostic confusion is in its desire to divorce truth from evidence, love from responsibility, sexuality from procreativity, dignity from innocence, souls from bodies, beliefs from creeds, churches from structures, and the Creator from his creation. For the Christian, the flesh is as much a mystery as the spirit; for Gnostics and their "New Age" counterparts, the body is a puzzle that is resolved by a quicksilver assertion of the autonomous self: "I can do what I want with my own body."

In the order of capital sins, pride comes first as the willful mistake about the soul. As humility is honesty about the self and creation, pride is the fundamental and deadly denial of the facts of life. Standing before the fact of the one true God, pride falls for the promise of ourselves becoming gods; he who is singular, pride pretends is plural. And since the ego is a very weak thing the more it stands apart from God, the Gnostic would energize it with a force drawn from a mythical evil equivalent of God, a dark energy in perpetual and unpredictable conflict with the God of Light. When Christ says, " . . . many that are first will be last, and the last first" (Mt 19:30; Mk 10:31; Lk 13:30), pride replies, "I'm Number One." When Christ says, "If any man would come after me, let him deny himself and take up his cross and follow me" (Mt 16:34; Mk 8:34), pride replies, "I've got to be me." And when Christ says, "He who abides in me, and I in him, he it is that bears much fruit, for apart from me you can do nothing" (Jn 15:5), pride answers, "I can do anything I want."

A Harmony Undone

The harmony of creation vanishes when perception is so completely turned upside down. Few composers have the heart for authentic symphony when the Divine Love that made the world is obscured by illusion. Love turned upside down becomes narcissism, plaintive Echo falls on deaf ears making noise, the cacophony of a society tone deaf to God. "About this we have much to say which is hard to explain, since you have become dull of hearing" (Heb 5:11). True music, as the highest of the arts, expresses purity and humility and devotion. But in a convoluted social order, music contradicts itself by hymning impurity. It degrades the gift of sexuality by abandoning the poetry of reticence, and admits ultimate failure by recourse of its performers to morbid androgyny. It defies the virtue of humility by becoming a sonic massage of the ego: the louder the better, and the more intrusive to the sensibilities of others the more amusing. It abandons any devotion by exalting brutality and sadism; it confounds sociability and promotes passivity by its sheer unsingability; it has no finale but ends in a fading repetition, and so insinuates absurdity. Aristotle did not hesitate to call this kind of orgiastic and aimless rhythm "slave music". The only commercial classical radio station in Los Angeles has gone out of business because, according to the management, there were not enough listeners in that vast population who could follow a symphony to its conclusion. Each biography has a Genesis, yet there are fewer by the day who can follow the symphonic quality of their lives to a Revelation. Lives are patterns of themes, but when they conclude in a void, they become surrealist echoes of the primal Voice saying to the first sea and first earth: "Let there be life."

Virtually no derivative song is adequate to say all that God wants said. "If I speak with the tongues of men and of angels, but have not love, I am a noisy gong or a clanging cymbal" (1 Cor 13:1). Human attempts at harmony apart from God introduce a lament, and paradisiacal pictures are painted with melancholy: the neoclassicists meant *Et in Arcadia ego* to be an ironic epitaph. On the human stage, in deprecating analysis, the third age of life admits the wistfulness of natural longing:

> And then, the lover,
> Sighing like a furnace, with a woeful ballad
> Made to his mistress' eyebrow.

We are back to the sentiment that offers itself as ransom for hostage truth, the supposition that feeling and symbol exhaust the meaning of faith, and that religion is something like emotional putty to fill in the cracks where reason is missing. But it is not so in Scripture, and King Solomon's "largeness of heart" was his wisdom, and not a counterweight to wisdom. At the beginning of the nineteenth century the theologian Schleiermacher offered in the kindliest of spirits his patronizing definition of religion as "sensibility and taste for the infinite". There is even a suspicion that spiritual longing is a pathological sublimation of failed romance, though this defies the entire architecture of saintliness. The lives of the saints show in brilliant ways how romance is an allegory of religious longing, and how this longing is the most reasonable of pursuits because it is in steady pursuit of the truth.

Authentic religious music, then, is not exploitive. It is neither agitative nor voluptuous, neither Hypophrygian nor Hypolydian in the terminology attributed by the sixteenth-century monk Glareanus to the Greeks. They had the psychological sense to identify the modes of music according to their ethical effect on the personality; it evokes sentiment as a proper endowment of love but conforms it to reason in a measured and meditative way. Reforming popes like Saint Gregory I and Saint Pius X have ardently condemned trivial, maudlin, and meretricious musicality in sacred worship as offenses against ascetic, and not just aesthetic, integrity in the sacramental order of creatures; and the Second Vatican Council repeated the particular appropriateness of Gregorian chant for the theological character of the Roman liturgy. Indeed, there is nothing truly aesthetic that is isolated from ascetic obligations to truth. Music that makes words peripheral is not liturgical; there is no such thing as "background" liturgical music for this reason.

Bearing in mind Kierkegaard's dictum, " . . . music in relation to the spoken word is both the leader and the follower, coming both first and last", there has to be a constant care for balance between the appeal to emotion, which fosters passivity, and the appeal to reason, which fosters activity. When the liturgy is passive it is entertainment, and only when it elicits the active assent of the intellect can it claim to be worship. In a purely ethical framework, both in *The Republic* and his *Laws,* Plato condemned the inherent degeneracy of music that functions only as entertainment. As the guardian and fulfillment of the ethical tradition, the collective prayer of the Church requires the faithful to think as they sing, and to think right things. Otherwise the human race is left naked in the universe, divorced from its dignity as steward of creation; just as, said Chesterton in his *Autobiography,* "dividing the tune from the words of a song" is a definition of divorce between husband and wife.

That Which Is Perfect

Human souls in their imperfection, bearing the ancestral wound of Adam's unfinished reason, love partially. Though we are in the image of God, the mirror is dark. The most Arcadian of human nuptials must still respect the sobriety of the prospect "til Death do us part". But when love is consecrated to its source, through holy vows of obedience to the Divine Love, then it moves from transporting embrace to transcendent union. Christian marriage and Holy Orders thus become indissoluble, and only functional disharmony within creation would presume to make them transient. When all others in the Passion of Christ toyed with unfaith and irreason, purity and humility and devotion in the figures of the Blessed Lady and the Beloved Disciple remained at the foot of the cross. Theirs could not quite be called the highest form of love; it is, so far as we can say, the only form of love. The legitimate though lesser forms of love, those friendly and erotic and affectionate as we know them, are more like notes and passages excerpted from the score of which this holy love is the whole and high blast.

When Saint Paul declaims from his apostolic stage there is none of the sloth of Shakespeare's Jaques in him, none of the wistfulness of the lovesick swain, none of the spiritual anemia rouged as sophisticated world-weariness. The Divine Romance between heaven and earth makes little fabrications of romance fugitive and very weak by comparison: "Love never ends; as for prophecies, they will pass away; as for tongues, they will cease; as for knowledge, it will pass away. For our knowledge is imperfect and our prophecy is imperfect; but when the perfect comes, the imperfect will pass away" (1 Cor 13:8–10).

Perfect love is almost by definition an abstraction in a culture that assumes it cannot exist. Can it exist? It is certain that it cannot even be intimated by temporary arrangements that simulate love. "Therefore a man leaves his father and his mother and cleaves to his wife, and they become one flesh" (Gen 2:24). Love cannot attain to perfection when it contradicts its fecundity by contracepting life. "I came that they may have life, and have it abundantly" (Jn 10:10). Nor can love gaze upon perfection when it qualifies itself with escape clauses and prenuptial agreements: "What shall a man give in return for his life?" (Mt 16:26; Mk 8:27) And love to be blessed by perfection cannot be divorced: "For your hardness of heart Moses allowed you to divorce your wives, but from the beginning it was not so" (Mt 19:8; Mk 10:5). The human heart apart from the Divine Love can be hard as nails. On Good Friday, those who had been blind until his hands touched their eyes could see the nails enter his hands; and those who had been deaf until his hands touched their ears could hear the hammering upon the nails. Hatred alone did not haul our Lord up into position on the cross. Cynicism and disappointment and cowardliness mortally reproached him and helped to knock his joints against the wood. The hateful heartless cannot be hard-hearted; hardness of heart is the disease of the half-hearted. By half-love is love crucified.

The less conditional love is, the more it is given to chorus and song. And hearts in love with God sing best. So the Second Vatican Council described the Church's liturgy as the world's delectation of heaven; and if it does not invariably seem so in the parish it is because the

dialogue of heaven and earth has been drowned out by
the ego arguing with itself, and if attempts at beauty
become contrived it is because the aesthetic has been
skimmed away from the ascetic like icing off the cake, not
absentmindedly or lazily, but pridefully in the conceit that
beauty can live without holiness.

> In the earthly liturgy we take part in a foretaste of that
> heavenly liturgy which is celebrated in the Holy City of
> Jerusalem toward which we journey as pilgrims, where
> Christ is sitting at the right hand of God, Minister of the
> holies and of the true tabernacle. With all the warriors of
> the heavenly army we sing a hymn of glory to the Lord;
> venerating the memory of the saints, we hope for some
> fellowship with them; we eagerly await the Saviour,
> Our Lord Jesus Christ, until he our life shall appear and
> we too will appear with him in glory (*Sacrosanctum
> Concilium,* no. 8).

The Holy Week of the year is the fountain of the
Church's entire musical life, housing its most venerable
and encompassing songs; no surprise that, for it is all about
what has been done to us by the world's First Lover, and
when his sound is heard from the cross it is clear that he is
anything but lovesick. To coin a phrase from a heavenly
treasury, Christ is lovestrong. Not once in the three hours
of agony does he emit a false note and, marvelous to say, as
the hours move along his voice actually sounds louder. It
has forced the saints to sing and has made the unlikeliest of
them perfect balladeers. Some of the noblest lyrics in the
Church's golden repertoire were authored by a man who
did not look like a lover. Saint Thomas Aquinas did not
lend himself to portraiture, and he seems to have exhausted
the sculptors; but statuary never was the best medium for

showing that saints do not have hearts of stone. He sang songs still sung seven centuries later: "Lauda Sion", "Pange Lingua", and if the records are correct, "Adoro Te", too. They are so austere and lustrous in their economy of thought that no word can be removed without losing the whole; and were you to ask this great saint why he spent his genius so, he would likely say that it was only a buzz in his ear from the most gaunt and shining sight the world has ever seen, nodding to Love Crucified. A vision less than that can only produce music less than that. When Monsignor Ronald Knox was asked why Modernist theologians do not write hymns like those of Saint Thomas, he replied, "Birds of prey have no song."

Christ in the Garden

Expect tension when one tries to sing in the maelstrom of imperfection. We are in a garden, this creation, but it has gone to seed. That was not its original condition, and for that reason original sin, or "original weediness" if you want, is a blight. To pretend that there is no original sin insults nature; it means that a blighted moral landscape is just an elegantly casual way of human horticulture, that rebellion and sickness and death belong in life the way volcanoes belong in parks. There is not a tone of that in the way Christ looks at his creation. He really is The Gardener and Mary Magdalen was not off the mark when she took him for one on Easter morning. He has come to confront what has deadened his garden, and finds straw in his own cradle and blood on his own tree. "Sir, did you not sow good seed in your field? How then has it weeds?" (Mt 13:27). It was not always thus, and long after this primeval rebellion it was the vocation of the Chosen People to preserve a memory of the verdant good in the form of a love song. Among the loveliest is one which was a prophecy:

> Whither has your beloved gone,
>   O fairest among women?
> Whither has your beloved turned,
>   that we may seek him with you?
> (Song of Solomon 6:1)

The answer, and really the point of the song, is that the beloved has "gone down to his garden". By the mystery of the Incarnation, God the Son looks upon his creation from within it, examining it with a body subject to created time and space; and still there is nothing lame and absurd in the way of the "woeful ballad". Time and space do not compromise his perfection, and indeed he has brought his perfection into creation to let it bloom again. Because nature is perfected in Christ, when justice without mercy would have meant its obliteration, divine science speaks of redemption rather than replacement. As he walks through some simple field on which the sun plays its ancient show of hours: "Consider the lilies of the field, how they grow; they neither toil nor spin; yet I tell you, even Solomon in all his glory was not arrayed like one of these" (Mt 6:28–29; Lk 12:27). He had that way of playing the changes of heaven as though he were tossing asides, what later people could call one-liners, walking along without losing a step; but one who looks that way at the flowers, and in this instance quite ordinary little wildflowers grandly called lilies in translation, has been looking at them a long time or, to tell the whole truth, from the time the first one ever appeared.

When he prepared to feed five thousand men, and a

vaster number of their families who did not figure into oriental statistics (cf. Mt 14:21), he arranged them like "garden beds" upon the "green grass". That is the literal meaning of the "groups" mentioned in most versions (Mk 6:40). The Evangelist Mark may mean to stress the colors in this human garden when he contrasts them with the green of the grass; he is not ordinarily as instinctive as Luke about mentioning such artistic details, and it obviously made a deep impression. You can hardly imagine Christ officiously sauntering through a botanical garden looking for a sensible color here and there; whatever he puts together, parables or events, seem to fit without effort, and here is a lesson for the harmony of races and clans and tongues, too.

Christ is a gardener and not a florist; he is not a fastidious arranger of things as though they might clash without the help of his good taste. It would have been quite unlike him to mutter: "Good Heavens, don't those marigolds look hideous next to the purple rhododendron?" Yet none of his most acidic critics, the tithers of dill and mint and cummin, accused him of vulgarity or a lack of sympathy; the harlequin crowds around him were a motley crew but, however much they contrasted with each other, they never seemed incongruous when they were near him. Once, let us remember, his promise was a rainbow, and his worst insult was to call certain people "whitewashed". It is really quite remarkable how no colors in creation clash until human meddling tries to sort them out according to human codes of balance and order. If the older Sadducees and Pre-Raphaelites and newer snobs and eugenicists have ears to hear, let them hear this noble whimsey whispered over the tall grass of Galilee.

As the Son of God could see a king's ransom in the

pollen of little more than a weed, he can see the King himself in a human soul. An Australian priest was teaching the parable of the lost sheep to a group of children at a sheep station. He asked them what their own fathers would do if among all the flocks one lone sheep went wandering at night in a storm. One boy raised his hand: "He'd let the little blighter go." It was not the textbook answer, though it was the natural answer and reminded the priest of the neglected mystery of Christ's story: the best shepherds are still only human, but the Good Shepherd is from heaven and sees more than others. He alone will walk through the labyrinths of centuries and lengths of continents to seek the one last sheep that is lost.

The strongest faith finds that hard to understand and certainly not the way to do business. But Christ's perfection does not include the virtue of faith, for he does not have to trust in the unseen: Christ, as we have heard the testimony, sees all things, and even when he looks at our hearts he is enjoying the Beatific Vision, and when he looks from the manger and from the cross and from the clouds on Olivet he sees through them to his Father in Heaven. "No man ever spoke like this man!" (Jn 7:46) because no man ever saw what this man saw. "And he looked at him . . . " (Jn 1:42). It is even harder to translate how he sees without a glossary of possibilities: he looked closely (Rieu), looked fixedly (Knox), looked hard (Jerusalem), gazed (Moffatt). The account he gives of what he sees is, in a higher sphere, a song to a world long grown tone deaf to the sound and blind to the sight.

He knows that each time fallen man tries to sing alone there will be a nervous and jarring note. To reach for a height will mean to be daunted one way or another. A plant will stretch to the sun, but it also may wither in the sun; and flesh that basks in the sun also can burn in the sun. A fawn may pant for the water brook but also can drown in it. Here is the ground of compassion, and wonderful it is to recognize that it moves the Creator who has "neither parts nor passions" to involve himself to the degree of the holy Passion of the Cross.

Of all the sacred types of the way this Passion plunges into broken beauty to birth it again, none shimmers more on the page like an illumination than the story of Joseph. Jacob loved Joseph above all his other sons and made him a coat of many colors. This delighted Joseph and pleased his father even more while the brothers grew jealous. They sold Joseph into bondage and dipped the coat in the blood of a goat. Jacob was handed the coat, stained with what he thought was the blood of his son, and mourned, covering himself with ashes. God the Father has clad his Son in a coat colored with the splendor of temporal creation, and this world has dipped it in the blood of Life. The charge of man against God becomes the charge of God against man: "For he crushes me with a tempest, and multiplies my wounds without cause . . . " (Job 9:17). The Divine Father is impassible, beyond suffering, but in his infinite majesty he sees earth as the Son sees heaven and bids the order of inanimate creatures to mourn its offended harmony. On history's longest Friday, the breeze cried and the sky put on ash, cleft and gray.

The Woman in Creation

Imperfect love finds its one remedy in the Love that has not failed, and as perfect Love humbles himself to become a man, he requires a mother; and as true humility is not condescending, he requires a perfect mother, and as perfect grace is not derivative he requires a virgin mother. Once he asked a crowded room: "Who is my mother, and who are my brethren? . . . whoever does the will of my Father in heaven is my brother and sister, and mother" (Mt 12:48, 50; Mark 3:33, 35; Lk 8:21). Something more warranted than conjecture enables the Church to think he may have turned a glance to his mother standing outside the window and smiled; for she is the only one of God's creatures who did perfectly and well the will of his Father. Perfect obedience becomes the infallibility of the Church that, unlike neuter institutions, is our holy Mother, never accurately "it" and properly "she": "Maria-Ecclesia" and "Ecclesia-Maria".

From the cross then he calls her Woman before he calls her Mother; perfect obedience makes her the universal helpmate and companion of a world orphaned by rebellion. "Woman, behold your son" (Jn 19:26). He is leaving Love on earth by the power of the Holy Spirit, and as Love needs a mother so the mother needs to love; the ephemeral children whom the Perpetual Virgin loves have surrendered the hill bellowing their moral chaos, leaving John in crystalline silence as her sudden new son. And joined with him from that moment will be as many as are willing to brave his innocence, which is like plunging into the eye of a storm and sliding over an impalpable rainbow both at once. Mary turns to John, and the universal quality of Mary's claim upon the human race is asserted. She is the head of all nature obedient to the will of the Beloved, and thus she is able to declare what on the lips of any other woman is harsh and false: "I am Woman!"

As one of the three Persons of the Holy Trinity, Christ is begotten, or bestowed to creation; not made, or invented by the initiative of creation. And human claim upon Mary as Mother, nurturer in the way of salvation, comes through obedience to the will of her only begotten Son. Conformity of the conscience to the doctrines of the Church is deeper than the shoals of legal requirement and the fatal exactitudes of rules; such obedience is alive when it loves the Mother who never lies. There is from his heart on the cross a song such as we cannot understand apart from the truths spoken through the Church: "Behold your mother." The maternity of the Church means that she is most clearly supernatural when she is human; her absolutions are most powerful against the gates of hell when on the lips of weak priests; her teaching most clearly the will of our Father in heaven when defined by one childless man in Rome.

It is a common expression that we do not need to go through a man to God; and it would be true, except that God went through a man to us. "For it was from the side of Christ as he slept the sleep of death upon the cross that there came forth the wondrous sacrament of the whole Church" (*Sacrosanctum Concilium,* no. 5). To profess no need for an institutional Church is to boast no need for the womb of Mary and the cross of Christ; the Church was instituted nowhere else. "You will be a son of thunder if you are a son of the Church; since from the gibbet of the cross Christ may say to you also: 'Behold thy mother'; and also he may say to the Church: 'Behold thy son': it is then that you will begin to be a son of the Church, when you shall see Christ victorious on his cross . . . " (St. Ambrose, *Exp.* LC. viii).

Christ was the one victim in the record of history who sang a love song while being crucified, sung to his Church and never ending: exultingly when popes are enthroned and the weight of the gospels is placed on the shoulders of

bishops at their consecration; stirringly when saints are
lashed and imprisoned and put away from human sympathy;
mournfully when the baptized lose heart and fall by the
wayside; and most happily when the blessed give shelter to
the poor who have lost their home and to the philosophers
who think there is no home. To be sure, the Church will
have an up and down history, and it cannot be otherwise
since from the hours on the cross the history of the Church
will be the history of creation, and anything not of the
Church will be in the order of commentary. The vicissitudes,
the "ups and downs" are foreseen from the cross in their
totality. When others turn their backs to the cross and
walk away, John turns his face to Mary: "And from that
hour the disciple took her to his own home." The home is
his conscience, and by taking Mary there, the conscience
always free is her conscience. Thus the truly free conscience is formed by the obedience of her in whose womb
Christ himself was formed.

Christ mottled in blood is the same who considered the
lilies of the field in their array. As his corpse is lowered and
returned to the Woman to be embalmed, she gives full
vent to what once was a hinted theme beautiful in its
melancholy:

> My beloved has gone down to his garden,
>   to the beds of spices,
> to pasture his flock in the gardens,
>   and to gather lilies.
> I am my beloved's and my beloved is mine;
>   he pastures his flock among the lilies.
>   (Song of Solomon 6:2–3)

The song is about living even more so because it is in
the presence of rigid death, and this sets it apart from the

lovely wistfulness of laments and panegyrics before and since. There is not least of all the fabled phrase in Holinshed's *Chronicles* by which Mary Tudor acknowledged the place of one embattled city in her political fortunes: "When I am dead and opened, you shall find 'Calais' lying in my heart." History and civility do well never to forget fine sentiments like that, noble antiques; but they also creak like antiques. It is different with the heart of the Woman. That heart was not exhausted by any age or place, and each sword that bitterly opened it revealed an ageless mirth. From delectable mountains grace brought to the Woman the long lost art of humility, and she became its gallery. The same grace assumed her to heaven, body and soul, incorrupt and intact. By recollection, though that should suffice, the world can still inspect her Immaculate Heart at the foot of the cross and see its tenant, the name Jesus, which she has made love's longest song.

CHAPTER FOUR

THE SOLDIER

"My God, my God, why hast thou forsaken me?"

Hysterics and Heroes

B Y A LAW of human nature more frequently observed than not, words hysterical or heroic fall from the lips of those about to be executed. There is the high and almost gothic hysteria of the innocent who do not understand why or how it is happening. "A voice was heard in Ramah, wailing and loud lamentation, Rachel weeping for her children; she refused to be consoled, because they were no more" (Mt 2:18; cf. Jer 31:15). These cries take long in fading and become aches that harrow others all their lives. There are the screams of the guilty piercing the halls of every century; anonymous malefactors and notorious tyrants who spy their approaching hour, trying to flee and shrieking like stuck pigs as they are shot or stabbed. You can see it on news programs as the television flashes warnings to a public unaccustomed to attending traditional morality plays. When cold death used crosses, rags sometimes were stuffed into the criminals' mouths to stifle their blasphemies. Now you need only turn your dial to another channel.

Heroism is a more curious unpredictability, not explained in every case as philosophical stoicism, or pessimistic resignation, or the cultivated style of a "stiff upper lip". There is the heroic shout of souls ablaze with honor supernaturally refined, whose last sounds gild the tawdriness around them. Sometimes it is the spontaneous heroism born in the last moment; of King Charles I led to the scaffold it could be said as Malcolm said that "Nothing in his life became him like the leaving it" (cf. *Macbeth* I. iv. 7).

For others the last moment is the triumph of a lifelong habit; about the year 107 Bishop Ignatius of Antioch said in his white hairs, "I am God's grain and I am to be ground by the teeth of wild beasts that I may be found the pure bread of Christ." In 1535, Bishop John Fisher, aged beyond his less than seventy years by illness and mortifications and imprisonment, flicked away his walking stick as he approached the steps leading to the chopping block: "I can manage the last few steps on my own." A shining few saved their last jokes for the great moment, like Thomas More trying to make the lieutenant smile, and the nun Pelagia Bles in the French Revolution distributing a box of sweets, "For my wedding". And some like Father Pro and his companions in Mexico shouted in fiery Spanish their *"Viva Cristo Rey!"*

Nor is the habit reserved to the resigned in years and long in formation. In the First World War, Paul Claudel said, "Youth is not made for pleasure but for heroism." Young youth, that is; since youth is new when it does not need pleasure to be happy; only the old think of the pleasures of youth. In the early Christian persecutions a very young shepherd Sozon was forced to walk about for hours with nails driven through his feet, when he then stood in his own blood and said to the magistrate, "I have finer red shoes than you!" In the nineteenth century some Ugandan lads refused to submit to the depraved pleasures of their King Mwangu and, with arms hacked off, they sang as they lay over slow flames; they sang a missionary translation of the hymn trilled by boys in sunny boarding schools far away: "Daily, daily sing to Jesus".

Though all the virtues did not abide heroically in Louis XVI, he went to his death in a regal way with consequences attendant upon the death of any true king. A century before, Corneille, in whose plays the only heroes really were heroes, said with sober prophecy, "The blow by which kings fall causes a long bleeding." This King's patrimony was great, being the heritage of France that had known crowned saints, and when he died in simple dignity, posterity was warned of a shining inheritance that cannot be spent. The Abbé de Firmont is supposed to have cried out at the fatal reckoning: "Son of Saint Louis, ascend to heaven!" And all that valor and faith flowed from the One whose kingdom was not of this world. When Christ was nailed, the Prince of Lies unmasked the false consolations with which he has been seducing God's creatures since the creation of the first soul. Satan, so far as it is possible to put into human words the unearthly dialogue of life and its contradiction, whispered into the ear of the Prince of Peace: "Son of God, go to hell!"

The Mocker. The Tempter. Getting in his last digs. Jesus is not hysterical. Even in this crucible of pain he has the recollection to call on God, singing a scripted psalm, the twenty-second, though with an intimacy that would petrify human theological reflection, and his intellect crafts the appeal as a question: "My God, my God, why hast thou forsaken me?" (Mt 27:46; Mk 15:34). Into the world has come a new way of dying that moves beyond the ranks of martyrdoms and heroism; edifying deaths are not supposed to include an intimation of abandonment. Most of those who have not already fled the scene now shake their heads and prepare to withdraw from conspicuous failure. By a confusion of languages in the din they assume he is calling on Elijah, the prophet of prophets. Well, let Elijah save him.

A Soldier's Oath

If he is neither hysterical nor heroic, what then is he, and
what manner of death can this be? Now it can be said,
strange though it is to say, that he is a soldier, and his moan
is a battle cry. The night before he had said to Peter, "Put
your sword back into its place; for all who take up the
sword will perish by the sword. Do you think that I
cannot appeal to my father, and he will at once send me
more than twelve legions of angels? But how then should
the scriptures be fulfilled, that it must be so?" (Mt 26:55;
cf. Jn 18:11). He has a sword, he who has "not come to
bring peace but a sword" (Mt 10:34; cf. Lk 12:51): he is the
sword himself. And the battle, feeling the frame of human
vision, is that far and deep encounter to which he alone is
admitted, in the solitude of the high priest whose singular
privilege was to enter the Holy of Holies on behalf of the
whole House of Israel one solemn day of the year; however Christ must enter alone the threshold of the unholy.
Other campaigns and assaults, all of them on all the fields
of hard human conflict from the outskirts of Eden to
Stalingrad, are shadow pictures and line drawings of this
unspeakable encounter; and no mere human crusader can
attempt so bold a siege and live.

> Then, a soldier,
> Full of strange oaths, and bearded like the pard,
> Jealous in honour, sudden and quick in quarrel,
> Seeking the bubble reputation
> Even in the cannon's mouth.

So that is a soldier like every other in heavy helmet, but
not like the one called Christ who fights on the wood of
the cross as a stark aboriginal burned by the sun. His

ragged beard is too caked with blood to see how it has outgrown fashion. And as for his jealous defense of honor, he only had that sad terrible look when the poor wood crown was pressed on his head; it is enough to recall the prayer of one venerable priest in a chapel of Madrid: "Lord, if you do not need my honour, what should I do with it?" Sheep are not sudden and quick in quarrel like soldiers, and "As a sheep led to the slaughter or a lamb before its shearer is dumb, so he opens not his mouth" (Acts 8:32; cf. Is 53:7). His lungs are too tight and tongue too bloated to speak more than seven lines, and these have no quarrel with anyone on earth. But there is one thing: the oath; like the soldier in the play he has a strange oath, so strange that centuries of didacts have not had the heart to abandon its original Aramaic and Hebrew. *Eli, Eli, lama sabachthani?*

The psalm begins in distress; not despair of objective faith, but torn and ragged despair "of life itself" (2 Cor 1:8). And it ends with a victorious blare of a trumpet torn from raw dawn. The beginning, though, is what matters; it would be too glib, and too theologically patchwork, to skip over the beginning to get to the happy ending. This is not a prologue the actor is obliged to get through to reach the cheerier bit. The end triumph is cast first in the despair, as the trophies brought from the battlefield seal the anxious pageant of the first alarm when horses and men glisten together in the waiting.

The insinuating Evil One has been whispering, "Go to hell!" And he whispers it in weaker ways to each of us who are easily tempted because he wants us there, too, in the heart of meaninglessness. But suddenly it flashes upon his darkness that after the countless equivocating ways men have toyed with his offer, the Perfect Man is taking him seriously. Jesus is consciously approaching the threshold of hell. He who has seen Jesus has seen the Father, and Satan must panic for he is about to see Jesus at his own infernal gates. The malignant mind haunted by the memory of heaven is about to glimpse it; for Satan, who makes his home in hell, the prospect of heaven is positively hellish and a form of hell itself. And in reply to the hideous whisper, Christ cries out as the only one who knows how far hell has always been from heaven. "He disarmed the principalities and powers and made a public example of them, triumphing over them in him" (Col 2:15).

Christ suffers physically because the creation for which he suffers has offended God physically in a cataract of twisted ways. But for the sacrifice to be complete, he suffers also in the mind where, in lesser men, the most raucous rebellions are. In the dark recesses of the imaginative intellect he suffers for human indifference, self-love, secret pride, and unmortified passions. When his consciousness looks toward the vision that has been his uncreated joy, it perceives the encroaching edges of a created vacuum. The disciples take note of it one way, the executioners and their collaborators another. Compromised intelligence is embarrassed by this when it is sympathetic, like the disciples; or sneers at it when it has no shred of sympathy, like the accusing crowd.

This is the kinetic moment when the mutual obligation of faith and reason is beside the point; when an experience of isolation enters within the eternal unity of God the Son and God the Father, divine mystery becomes the conundrum it was never supposed to be. Only angelic intelligences have the capacity to be purely astonished at it, in a way that makes human sweat and tears by comparison frivolous as glass chimes. And the modern difficulty with the doctrine about angels has had the sorry effect of shrinking the modern ability to be astonished by anything greater than trinkets and second-rate cleverness. To allow the crudest analogy, as a poor wine will offend a winetaster more than a winebibber, so an interlude of darkness will be more shattering to the Light of the World than to those in his image who see "through a glass darkly", those nice enough types who think they see clearly enough when they see through the smoke of a good cigar; and an intuition of disunity will rack the Begotten One more than his creatures who are made and not begotten.

Christ cannot lose faith or hope since he never had them; his Incarnation, as we saw from his infancy, possessed the Beatific Vision that consummates and eliminates those two virtues. And he cannot lose love, as that is what he is. But he can sacrifice the unity between what he is and why he is, the identity of his being and his essence. He is the I AM; but in this despairing moment he becomes the consummate AM I?, bearing the full historical weight of existential crises. If lovers ache when they are bereft, Love himself must endure something for which there is no tolerable human term when he actually becomes Bereftment.

While fallen man dies as the consequence of sin, Christ dies as the consequence of ineffable holiness; and in effect, while we experience death as consequence, Christ endures death as cause: "And I saw, and behold, a pale horse, and its rider's name was Death, and Hades followed him . . ." (Rev 6:8). The most we can say, and we never say it very well, is that God is "angry" when human creatures do not worship this marvel. He is "angry" in justice whenever spectators stand in the shadow of the Passion and say breezily with Millais that life is "one damned thing after another". Worship raises men to the status of participants in the divine drama. To deny the anger of God at our willfull obtuseness, to pass off the concept of divine wrath as naïvely anthropomorphic, betrays our incomprehension of the dignity he accords us by the magnificence of his anger.

The despair of life, which is the failure of mortal men, is the final triumph of the Son of God. He is doing what he came to earth to do. There is something almost functional about his grief, not that it is unreal. Indeed, its authenticity is unmatched: "Look and see if there is any sorrow like my sorrow which was brought upon me . . ." (Lam 1:12). The psychology of meaninglessness has an awful meaning of its own; psychology becomes theology when the desolation is deliberate. When Christ insisted on going to Jerusalem he intended to enter that powerful darkness of absurdity on the cross (cf. Lk 22:53); and when he prayed that the cup would pass from him it was only because it reflected the inevitability of this mental thirst. As the human sense of meaninglessness gives birth to sorrow, the divine sense of sorrow destroys it; but only by being genuine anguish, not mitigated to any degree by its having been willed. And in the eucharistic sacrifice of the altar, where the sacrifice of Calvary once offered is fully present, the divine agony becomes the sublime hope of the world. For at the altar the human race is no longer a spectator of the absurd, but a participant in the conquest of the absurd "through him, with him, in him" whose greatest power is in his ability to die out of moral obedience rather than natural necessity, opposite the normal human process. This death actually manifests a power. Mere humans only have a power to live until death, but the God-Man has power to die, just as he has power to live again (John 10:18).

For Christ, to perceive the plausibility of meaninglessness is an act of obedience, introducing a tension in his soul far more painful than our experiences of abandonment precisely because his soul cannot be bereft of the Beatific Vision (S Th. III. q.46, a. 7). Where our agony is a paradigm of sin, his agony is a paradox of blessedness. In that sense it may be said, though most cautiously and analogically, that by subjecting himself to an exhaustion of the inexhaustible Beatific Vision, he was making the one act of faith and hope in his entire life. "Now faith is the assurance of things hoped for, the conviction of things not seen" (Heb 11:1). By losing sight of a sight that cannot be lost, an impossible play on words has become a cataclysmic play on life; and for one appalling moment, that which for man is a theater of the absurd is for the God-Man neither theatrical nor absurd. The virtuous consolations of faith and hope are his most painful abasements and become his ultimate servitude for our sakes and similitude to our moral condition. By having no faith or hope to lose, the desolation on the cross, the climax of his struggle as the "Yes" of God (cf. 2 Cor 1:18–20), is the harrowing exercise of faith and hope that are invoked for this one temptation to become "No" to the Father, who has ordered him to be so tempted (Jn 10:18).

Exactly in this maelstrom is the most radical activity of his priestliness and sacrifice, as though by a breathtaking symbiosis of providence and suspense: "For we have not a high priest who is unable to sympathize with our weaknesses, but one who in every respect has been tempted as we are, yet without sinning" (Heb 4:15). Each saint has charted this compelling and violent pattern: the heart of the passion and center of the sacrifice is located in the intersection of total sinlessness and the ultimate temptation.

Where the mind denies the priesthood of Christ, it becomes an acolyte of the absurd. By philosophizing, Nietzsche claimed precisely that, promising that the death of God would be the freedom of man, but this free man was only a bloated man contradicting himself: "I teach you the superman. Man is something to be surpassed." There are such thinkers who have so rearranged their mental furniture that they are convinced they have reordered the mansions of reality. At the end of his rewriting the will of God, Nietzsche sat down to his piano, and as his fingers tried to play the keys he went mad.

> The mind is its own place, and in itself
> Can make a Heav'n of Hell, a Hell of Heav'n.
> (Milton, *Paradise Lost,* I)

Nietzsche at the piano is an icon of the failed modern denial of God. The modern soul boasted of the superman as a way of hiding a fear of history, and history broods with warnings the superman would not hear. Christ has accorded men the sublime courtesy of coming to them as true God and true Man, and not as a superman who would have been either a toy god or a comic man. And when he came into history, the clear logic of what he said overwhelmed the illogic of what limited man thought he should say; just as the course of history rolls wave upon wave in unwitting testimony to this, in his day despite themselves, "so many thousands of the multitude had gathered together that they trod upon one another" (Lk 12:1). And so, too, as a new millennium approaches alight with variety, hysterics and heroes in all aspects of culture are pushing and shoving each other for a fresh glimpse of the God who was declared dead by modern madmen, disagreeing on points but at least agreeing in principle on one point, that man was not meant for madness unless it is the madness of heaven's own logic.

> If they have called the master of the house Beelzebul, how much more will they malign those of his household. So have no fear of them; for nothing is covered that will not be revealed, or hidden that will not be known. What I tell you in the dark, utter in the light; and what you hear whispered, proclaim upon the housetops. And do not fear those who kill the body but cannot kill the soul; rather fear him who can destroy both soul and body in hell (Mt 10:25–28).

Radical Warfare

Only the shedding of blood can cancel the moral oblivion that has been transmitted by blood since the first rebellion against Life. Sin is not an option for men, for the human condition of rebellion against God is not optional. Individual sins are choices, but sin itself originates in the rebellion of the first humans against their innocence. And thus Providence elects the shedding of innocent blood originating outside this ancestral denial of God to cleanse from sin the fragile human fact of our personality.

Battles against lesser evils are fought widely on a broad front: general theories of science assail ignorance of physical systems, and farflung ramparts are built against alien terrain; but the battle against the source of evil is acute and local as a needle, penetrating pride with innocence deeply rather than widely. The heavenly Creator then chooses to become more specific than theories have expected him to be; the original Innocence shuns the collective form of a nation or a race to become one particular man. By his own design, God is quite incapable of seeing crowds, let alone being one. He is the "One who Is" and sees only individuals; even when he feeds multitudes, he does not stave off hunger so much as satisfy the many particular hungers of many particular men gathered together. You can fancifully and poetically read "Christ figures" into any imaginary drama; in the authentic play of creation and re-creation, the original Innocence drinks from a cup and eats from a plate and sails one boat when he comes to confront the earthly rebellion. Divine deliberation meets it face to face; it would totally misrepresent the drama were it faces to faces.

Since the rebellion originates in time, the innocence intervenes from timelessness. The human story begins "in the beginning" but Christ already "*was* in the beginning" (cf. Jn 1:1). The *Eli, Eli lama sabachtani* has its power from the eternal innocence of the One who cries it. To speak of power here is to mean its prophetic urgency for those individual experiences of depression that are the common lot of human reflection and for those social experiences of desolation that set the tone for certain periods of culture. The confidence in progress as inevitable in nineteenth-century industrialized society sat tenuously on an intimation of the aimlessness of that progress; and because its romanticism was a substitute for the Divine Romance, it harbored a disturbing unquietness. When the cry of Christ was not heard, the poets were left to cry like elders sitting at the city gates. Matthew Arnold set to verse only what was pulsing in the veins of a whole segment of society. Of course he had the obligatory Victorian optimism:

Too quick despairer, wherefore wilt thou go?
   Soon will the high Midsummer pomps come on . . . "
(Thyrsis, 61ff.)

But so long as religion was "morality touched by emotion", as he held in the preening languor of his *Literature and Dogma,* reason had no solid hope beyond the fluff of optimism, and faith itself had no rational power to justify its justification of man. Its "melancholy, long, withdrawing roar" was louder than all the hymns to machines and self-improvement:

And we are here as on a darkling plain
Swept with confused alarms of struggle and flight,
Where ignorant armies clash by night.
(Dover Beach, 11:35ff.)

How odd, neither merely edifying nor surprising, to search and find none of this romantic pathos in the Passion of Christ. Even when the dark garden of his agony was swept with the "confused alarms" of the chief priests and captains of the temple and elders, there Christ was completely composed: "Have you come out as against a robber, with swords and clubs? When I was with you day after day in the temple, you did not lay hands on me. But this is your hour, and the power of darkness" (Lk 22:52–53). Even the disorder is part of an ordered plan, the way any battle strategy structures calamity; only here the strategy is of cosmic dimensions, and he has even calculated the legions of pure intelligences at his disposal (Mt 26:53). As armies go, this one is not ignorant by any means, and he hinted at the method of divine madness through the delicacy of a parable:

Whoever does not bear his own cross and come after me, cannot be my disciple. For which of you, desiring to build a tower, does not first sit down and count the cost, whether he has enough to complete it? Otherwise, when he has laid a foundation, and is not able to finish, all who see it begin to mock him, saying, "This man began to build, and was not able to finish." Or what king, going to encounter another king in war, will not sit down first and take counsel whether he is able with ten thousand to meet him who comes against him with twenty thousand? (Lk 14:27–32).

Jesus had prepared for the hour of darkness by an interior counsel of the Holy Trinity. He would have kept private his healing of the sick, for the time of confrontation had not yet come. At Cana he tells his Mother that his hour had not yet come. When Peter tries to block his way to Jerusalem, it is then that he cries out against the Satan at work in the bewildered fumbling of the Apostle, for the hour is growing closer. And when the time of agony finally arrived, faithful to its schedule, he sweat more feverishly than generals and prime ministers awaiting the invasion of some sinister beachhead. The detail is reserved to the clinical interest of Luke the physician: " . . . and his sweat became like great drops of blood falling down upon the ground" (Lk 22:44).

As pagan battles are in the hands of fate, this is in the hands of Providence. The difference is that fate robs one's freedom of action, and Providence gives the freedom necessary for the right action. The battle is won before it begins, then, and yet the action is as tenuous and tense as though nothing were assured. The Messianic declaration of the triumph takes a liturgical form now; this is the battle of a priest who is refining all of creation into a posture of worship: God bowing within the Godhead to show man how to bow before God. As the dismal fortunes of institutionalized atheism and inculturated materialism have shown most vividly in late modern times, it is not natural, and it is nearly by definition subhuman, for man not to worship. "I tell you, if these were silent, the very stones would cry out" (Lk 19:40).

Possibly the many generations since Descartes innocently spread the rumor of faith having been divorced from reason, and surely the last few generations have wondered why they should worship at all, and then they have begun to lose any sense of what worship in fact is, as though it were an arcane convention forced on people just to make them arbitrarily subservient. The truth, like all truths, is much more stimulating than wrong impressions of it: God's command to worship him is a privileged invitation to become more like his glory by bowing before it. God receives no increase in dignity when he is worshipped, but human creatures are incalculably enhanced by being allowed, indeed even commanded, to prostrate themselves before a source of being outside mechanical cause and effect within their own ecological chain. There is a whiff of healthy terror in the human capacity for worship when it is really exercised; there is nothing picturesque about the image of God in the soul.

Human excellence may come from outdistancing others of one's own species; human immortality comes from contact with the Immortal One. On the night of his betrayal, the divine etiquette of Jesus refrained from lecturing his faithful remnant on judicial reform or medical ethics or moral prudence. He was content in the parting moments before arrest to let them listen in as he lifted his eyes to heaven and uttered lines that the sacred texts properly keep in more formal diction than his colloquial conversations with them. No longer was he speaking to them. He was speaking in their presence, intoning as the High Priest of creation, interceding from earth to heaven on their behalf, but he was speaking to Another who had always been with him:

Father, the hour has come; glorify thy Son that the Son may glorify thee, since thou hast given him power over all flesh, to give eternal life to all whom thou hast given him. And this is eternal life, that they know thee the only true God, and Jesus Christ whom thou hast sent. I glorified thee on earth, having accomplished the work which thou gavest me to do; and now, father, glorify thou me in thy own presence with the glory which I had with thee before the world was made (Jn 17:1-5).

The Ongoing Battle

The inner dialogue of the Holy Trinity is the source and reference of all supernatural activity, and the validity of spiritual life depends on deference to it. To eavesdrop on the High Prayer of our Lord is to perceive from the highest parapets of grace the prelude to his victory: " . . . blessed are your eyes, for they see, and your ears, for they hear. Truly, I say to you, many prophets and righteous men longed to see what you see, and did not see it, and to hear what you hear, and did not hear it" (Mt 13:16-17; cf. Lk 10:23-24; Jn 8:56; Heb 11:13; I Pet 1:10-12; I Jn 1:1-2). But it is possible for moral obtuseness to reject the inner workings of the heavenly battle:

You shall indeed hear but never understand,
    and you shall indeed see but never perceive.
For this people's heart has grown dull,
    and their ears are heavy of hearing,
    and their eyes have closed,
lest they should perceive with their eyes,
    and hear with their ears,
and understand with their heart,
    and turn for me to heal them.
             (Mt 13:14-15; cf. Is 6:9-10)

The faithfulness of his own soldiers Christ fortifies with the enlistment of baptism, the commission of confirmation, the rations of the altar, the solidarity and increase of marriage, the leadership of the ordained, the healing of wounds in unction, and the absolution from sins that is the victory overcoming the world. But even an army so blessed can be decimated; soldiers can die as part of the winning, through the pervasive willfulness of others. An unprecedented number of men, women, and children have died for Christ in the twentieth century. Revolutions and high commands have knocked crosses off the shingled steeples and gilded domes of churches in nation after nation, grinding them into the dust. Self-commissioned armies have scorned the armies of Christ, asking like Stalin how many divisions the pope has, as once Christ himself was mocked by the Roman guards playing their hard game with him. And in some places they have tried to appropriate Christ's Body the Church for their own ends, as once they wrapped a soldier's cloak around the Nazarene for a joke. In the soldiers' barracks in Jerusalem, mental torture was for play; and the cat-and-mouse game played with Christ consisted in robing the victim and bowing before him as a king, hence the name Basileus for the game, and then stripping and beating him. Sometimes it would be repeated many times. How many divisions does the Man have? In these late times the answer is being given.

At the end of the Second World War when the people of Hungary cheered defeat of the swastika only to turn and find the hammer and sickle offending the walls, Cardinal Mindszenty gathered a vast crowd for pilgrimage and said to them:

Sin will never exercise perpetual power over any nation.

This reteaches us that everything on this earth is ephemeral whether it is the work of Genghis Khan, or of Napoleon or of Hitler. God sends the world scourges, an agony to try its soul, but relief is always waiting ahead, for the hand of the Lord is on history.

Four decades later, the Pope stood in Warsaw's Victory Square facing a vast crowd surrounded by the armed guards of a government about to be overthrown, and declared in approaching fulfillment of the Cardinal's prophecy: "You cannot keep Christ out of history!" In a civilization whose confidence in speculative theology has been shaken by impulsiveness, the idea of God in history has assumed its primitive mode as the sight of God in history. It can still be denied, but after amputating experience from being, by the willfully blind, and by moral characters too weak for so great a battle against evil.

From the foot of the cross when most of the civilian gawkers had deserted the scene, a soldier who remained out of obedience to orders stared, probably making little ethical sense of the spectacle, let alone giving it any theological thought. He was only doing his job. When the ground shook he saw that the crucified Man in his charge was dead, and some spontaneous thought came to him, that the Man had never really been in his charge or in any one else's. "Truly this was the Son of God" (Mt 27:54; Mk 15:39). Others evidently joined in, led by a soldier who had no business making public comments of any kind. But he was the one in the bedraggled group qualified to speak. That is to say, it takes a soldier to know a soldier and mark his rank.

CHAPTER FIVE

MIDDLE AGE

"I thirst."

The Mid-Life Crisis

COMPLACENCY is the silent enemy of life. A certain added menace attaches when it pretends to be inevitable and even desirable, in the Stoic tradition of detachment as an end in itself. Indifference to unworthy attachments and desires—for the sake of indifference—is falsely Christian piety; in natural philosophical form it reconstructs Stoic egoism in various modernized schools of self-affirmation techniques, and in pseudoreligious form it reconstructs Buddhist contempt for creation in some eclectic schools of "centering prayer" and Eastern meditation.

Neither Greek rigor nor Oriental placidity harmonizes with the Christian virtue of detachment for the sake of union with the Divine Lover of creation. The early Christians commended *apatheia,* and Saint Ignatius Loyola inspired a spiritual renewal with it as *indiferencia;* and it would tell much about the psychology of culture to trace how this genuine spiritual boldness gets supplanted by noiseless caricatures of detachment in the popular pathological forms of apathy and indifference. Nothing creeps into the souls more innocuously than this spiritual lethargy; complacency absorbs many meannesses and faults, but it is more than anything else a mood of occult sadness. It fools the self by offering many fleeting consolations and rewards, like physical prowess and professional prestige and political leverage or sometimes the perverse pleasure of finding one's subtle view of the world rejected by the vulgar masses; but these are distractions from the unhappiness

93

that complacency sneaks into the intellect and the will, and it is hard to complain because it all happens with a smile as though a pillow were being fluffed for the esteem of the inner man. Hatred bangs drums. Lust bangs the pulse. Anger bangs the fist. But complacency slides into the soul, unmurmuring, uninvited, and unnoticed, with a warm and quilted aura of coziness.

The complacent soul enjoys a certain measure of satisfaction secured by a massive ignorance of potentials, rather like Lord Kitchener's chief of staff in the Sudan, General Rundle, who "never took a risk, and was rewarded by never meeting a reverse". Now complacency is a particular bane of middle age. The young are too naïve for it; the old tend to be too anxious for it. Our Lord was about thirty-three when he died; the fullness and last bloom of youth. A good age, then; and a classical tradition thought everyone in heaven would have the age of their Redeemer, the Holy Innocents and the Living Elders alike. In his Fifth Word, Christ addresses that typical lassitude of spirit whose complacent mood is the ground of mid-life crisis, and this is only symbolically the midpoint of any one life. It is far more an address to the mid-life of any generation at the inevitable point when circumstances force it to confront the possible meaning of Christ's death. If his death has no significance greater than as a chronological point in history, then there is no point to history. The fact that some modern philosophies have based themselves precisely on the belief that it is pointless is not half so interesting as the utter failure of those philosophies to convince the most agile minds of the day; and by agile, one means more than the cleverest or most imaginative. One means the saintliest, and that is just a Frenchified way of saying the sanest.

Why a spectacular clump of centuries was called the

"Middle Ages" remains an enigma, at least to those who do not hold the relatively contemporary notion of our age as the ultimate age. The only ones who could possibly take the term literally would have to call classical times adolescent; but then they would also have to call the modern age geriatric, which they would never do. The very concept of modernity is a noticeably arrogant form of self-contradiction: claiming to be the final judge of a vast wisdom and the highest court of appeal for the ages, while being younger and more sprightly than any other age. The need to be modern is a complex of the aging; young people want to look older. The modern age made the fatal mistake, and the mistake typical of the complacent, of thinking it was young because it was new. You could say it was only late because it was new. Being recent does not connote youthfulness and certainly not innocence; it may only be the autumn after a summer, as the summer is a basking in some spring.

Now if that is so, the Middle Ages were far more like a springtime in which the Renaissance would bask, for the sixteenth-century classical revival is wrongly thought to have rebelled against the Middle Ages; it rather began a period far more like the middle age of a human life, after the youthful crusading and spiring of the Middle Ages. After all, mediaeval people were, from a modern point of view, scandalously young. As in every time until the most recent time, approximately one out of every three persons in the mediaeval period was under the age of fourteen. It is true that the mediaeval people, thought to be monstrously senile and antifeminist and everything bad, burned a nineteen-year-old girl at the stake, which we would be reluctant to do; it is also true that mediaeval people gave a seventeen-year-old girl command of an army, which we would be more reluctant to do. They had little sense of history, and even drew ancient figures in contemporary clothing working with the latest tools and stepping the latest dances; already in the twelfth century John of Salisbury warned that growing contempt for the past in favor of the new logic was unleashing an insolent childhood across the face of Christendom.

The Renaissance bankers and burghers, and no less the reforming divines, reflected on those insubordinate and unclassical years with some embarrassment, like waking up from a horrid Pied Piper dream. The humanists' solution was to forget it, as any therapist tells you to discount a nightmare; and then the reformers said it never happened, as if between the death of the last apostle and the birth of the first reformer there was a vast darkness when Christ went underground. It was high time to set up compact trade systems and the outlines of sensible territorial nations, to do the best they could to shut down those "Teen-Age" communes known as convents and charterhouses, and to dismantle or refine some of their architectural faux pas that screamed such barbaric contempt for the perfect proportions of the Augustan Age. When they looked back on the most blatant extravagances of the thirteenth and fourteenth centuries, the flashing polychrome and flying buttresses and arches whose points jabbed at common sense and decency, they had only one term for it, worse than a moralist calling an adolescent an "acid head" or "punker", an insult unsurpassed for its connotation of wild arrogance and senseless taste, and the term was "Gothic".

The Renaissance social fabric institutionalized apathy about eternity by the device of a massive prejudice that scorned the past period as a pause in progress; and to this day the word mediaeval is used as an insult. We are even told by some modern thinkers who approve of filthy thoughts that mediaeval towns and townspeople were filthy, when they were as obsessed with baths as the Romans and would have been shocked by the perfumed filth of Versailles and the choking squalor in the "Black Country" of Victorian mill towns. Death was not reserved for the old, and you did not have to decline into it; mediaeval people tended to live too intensely, even to frenzy, to think of decrepitude, and what was ancient and monumental they wantonly plundered for their new extravagances; it was left to the Victorians to romanticize decay, and to the modern philanthropists to restore old towns. The mediaevals went on pilgrimage to living shrines; it would not have occurred to them to make Compostela a Williamsburg or Jerusalem a theme park. The youth of mediaevalism promoted the maypole and chase; but the renaissance of humanism was more reflective and built museums and zoos. There is nothing more typical of the mediaeval mind than the fair and nothing less typical than the archive. While printing was a mediaeval invention, the golden books of the age were hand painted with ground jewels for ink; only later were books printed on vast scale with ground coal for ink. People did not chase butterflies, for butterflies chased people; they proliferated like mosquitoes. Food was glazed with honey to look like gilded trinkets. Even old bones seemed alive and interesting to the mediaevals, and they searched for dead young saints as eagerly as our senior scholars search for dead old dinosaurs. The solemn humanists would satirize the way they dressed the holy relics and talked to them.

No time has been so misnamed as the Middle Ages; they had been flagrantly and unforgivably the "Teen Ages" of Western civilization, and Renaissance man with his paunch newly acquired from a more sedentary posture, paternally fingering his key chain of metal mined in a New World, decided to quash their excesses and to summon errant young Matthew back to the exchange tables. The Renaissance was the Middle Age of humanity apologizing for its misspent youth. The mediaevals instituted systematized trade balances based on bullion; the Renaissance turned this measuring rod into a disciplinary rod for cartels and nations. And in the most stolid places like Germany and Holland, remaining vagrants of the wildly catholic "Teen Ages" were sentenced by ominous judges to correction in an amorphous enterprise rather chillingly known as the Reformation.

The grand and efflorescent spirit of the Renaissance, separate from but intrinsic to the Reforming spirit, was like the middling years of a man's life, a surrender to practical sense. Fashion stopped copying extravagant mystics like Bernard of Cluny and Dominic and resuscitated older sobriety. The Reformers wanted the wisdom of Israel; for the humanists the model was republican Rome, with the result that when its effects had spread far enough and its own time has passed, Virginia planters were posing in togas and Lord Chesterfield was giving his son the same advice Cato had given his. But in each case the result was edifying, of the sort that drains the headiness of springtime out of the very air. Startling theological claims of the mediaevals came to be remembered as the gawkiness of pubescence; the age of faith became an age of superstition in the opinion of more world-weary intellectuals whose rise as humanists coincided with their rise as bourgeoisie, launching conglomerates instead of crusades. It is a supreme irony that the new delicacy that criticized the fraudulent

selling of indulgences was so indulgent toward the concept
of selling and invented a system that could sell whole
nations on the basis of borders and whole races on the
basis of skin.

We are now at the tail end of a culture rooted in
philosophical traditions whose one unity was a repudiation of everything mediaeval except its stained glass. And
the modern mentality has still not explained why ages
believed to have been so dark should be famous for their
windows. The emerging consciousness of a united Europe,
and even of a Catholic Europe, may repudiate the myth
about mediaeval delinquency. It was the one myth shared
by modern capitalist and Marxist, Protestant and atheist,
and made the modern age the last gasp of the middle age
of man. Something fresher will have to appear to prevent
old age, and it will have to be the youthfulness of faith
rejecting the complacency of disbelief. A newer form of
the mediaeval exuberance will be needed to revive the
humanity behind those institutions created in a few fast
centuries by men and woman long thought lethargic and
calcified: city planning, scientific method, organized labor,
social services, universities, women's dignity, regulated
banking, courtesy, formal diplomacy, cultural unity, and
parliaments heard by kings.

In 1944, in *La France contre les Robots,* Georges Bernanos
predicted a great restoration of the spirit of youth "on all
levels of thought and of action, both of Morals and of
Art". It has yet to come, and if it does it will expose our
contemporary "youth culture" as the exploited artifact of
cynics who corrupted youth with a geriatric lie against
God. When that happens, the symbol of youth will be the
symbol banned by indolent hearts when they tried to
smash the cathedrals of the world: for the symbol is the

crucifix that made the nations young. And when the new glass buildings of our cities lie broken, the brightest of all buildings still will be the glass house built by a mediaeval king as a shrine to shine around young Christ's crown of thorns.

Unjust Justice

There is a fifth age of man, says the Bard, for which an evolving universe is the stage, confident times like the Renaissance are allegories, and man is the vital fact:

> And then, the justice,
> In fair round belly, with good capon lin'd,
> With eyes severe, and beard of formal cut,
> Full of wise saws and modern instances;
> And so he play his part.

His use of "modern" is different from ours. The Elizabethan means "ordinary"; the man of the fifth age is a grand dispenser of commonplace information, a cracker-barrel philosopher with an ample flow of clichés for various sorts and conditions. Glibness is the diction of complacency. Today he might make a popular television commentator, or a pliable legislator, or even a cleric who confuses vocation with career. No profession is closed to him, no state of life, because unadvertised complacency can slip into the greatest as well as the meanest spirits; and there it nests waiting to see what we will do next. There is really nothing the complacent soul could not be except a just judge.

The middle-aged justice appears to be on top of almost everything in his grasp and purview. He is on top of the social order, first of all: he is a justice weighing that order in albeit tilted balances. He is on top of affluence; his fair round belly was in his day an envied testimony to that, as his cautious eye put him on top of sophisticated commentary, and his formal haberdashery put him on top of the understated elegance whose importance is overstated by the *parvenu*. Sustaining it all is a gift for "the easy speeches that comfort cruel men". He is on top of nearly everything, as those who master the ways of complacency often can be, securing high places by virtue of their accommodating innocuousness, laureled leaders in a tyranny of mediocrity. He boasts to camouflage an inferiority complex founded in objective inferiority; and with ramshackle populism he criticizes excellence as elitism, a compliment when used as a pejorative by the envious. His insecurity adopts a mixed bag of poses: insincere obsequiousness, affected heartiness, feline duplicity, promotion of the common. In the panorama of positions and places, you will find the complacent in every alley and palace, but in the vastest continents the one place you will never find him is on top of a cross. No one is complacent on a cross.

Christ is anything but complacent there. The Judge of the World looks like no justice on that awful tribune; injustice has paraded him there. His sad silhouette traces no fair round belly. His eyes are severe only in the guilty perception; a few days earlier they cheered children who cheered him. His beard is grown long past formal cut; prisoners are not permitted blades. He has no wise saws and modern instances; it is hard to croak last words from parched lips, and his burning brain, which never entertained clichés, has no time for them when spinning in pain. And what then is the part he plays in middle age, midway between the old promises of God and their completion, in between earth and heaven? It is only the real play, uninteresting to the complacent who think themselves on top of the world and all the sadder for finding that not so high after all.

Once Jesus had been on the top of things. He once had been on top of the healing profession, and crowds came to seem him at it; now he is dying. He once was on top of the food business, feeding five thousand here and four thousand there; now he hungers. When he was on top of wine production at Cana, some remarked how well he did it; now he cries, "I thirst."

To Drink the Blood

When he began the few years of public life, three years at the most, he fasted forty days and forty nights. " . . . and afterwards he was hungry" (Mt 4:2). The Latin is as blunt as the Greek: *postea esuriit.* Some of the updated translations miss the Scriptures' marvelous power of understatement by corruptly reading he was "very hungry". Of course he was hungry beyond our ability to imagine, but the authentic text characteristically leaves this to the realm of the unsaid and even unspeakable. The modest Lenten fast is a pallid deference to the Messianic fast, and should we succeed in keeping it, there is still the danger of self-satisfaction that undoes the purpose of humbling the human spirit.

Our Lord began his ministry hungering, and he ends it thirsting, each part of the whole fabric of spiritual perfection: "Blessed are those who hunger and thirst after justice . . . " (Mt 5:6). When he turned water to wine in his first miracle, he had in mind the hour that was to come on the cross, intimated though not yet manifest. Now the hour has come, and as he cries in thirst, he gurgles blood. Jesus

Christ is drinking his own blood. His own body quenches his thirst. Let complacent souls look now at this, who deny that the Holy Eucharist is a sacrifice. Let complacent souls see what he is drinking, who think the chalice of the Blessed Sacrament the Eucharist is wine sentimentalized to memory and not wine consecrated to blood.

Someone watching the cross, a euthanasia man, does what a complacent world judges to be a charitable work by offering Christ a sedative or placebo on a sponge mixed with wine. The Living Truth did not come into the world to become anesthetized apathy; he presses his lips shut, keeping the promise made in the Upper Room: "I shall not drink of this fruit of the vine again, until I drink it with you, new wine, in the kingdom of my Father" (Mt 26:30). In a world that has anesthetized its consciousness of God until his barest mention becomes a painful violation of its moral slumber, the Lord hangs in display of what it is to thirst for true perfection.

One of history's most dangerously imperfect thinkers called religion the opium of the masses. As his credibility fades, it has become evident to many who once followed Marx that Christ's Church alone among the organs and institutions in the modern age has refused the opium of unreality. And that notwithstanding those numerous voices who in the name of their own fanciful Christianity have published books and advertised in the newspapers on behalf of a sedated Gospel and inflected theology. In these modernist misadventures, nuanced truth is drugged truth; and however they press it to his lips, Christ will spurn the sponge of such round-bellied indifference. And though he thirsts now two thousand years longer than he thirsted on the cross, he will not quench his holy passion with a moderated moral demand, a watered down priesthood, truncated vows, and vacant worship. Press these to his lips and he will not drink, not after two thousand years of modern instances stretched up to him will he drink. Press to his lips the claim that after these many centuries the human race has come of age on its own terms, and he will not drink such immature wine.

> I press on toward the goal for the prize of the upward call of God in Christ Jesus. Let those of us who are mature be thus minded. . . . For many, of whom I have often told you and now tell you even in tears, live as enemies of the cross of Christ. Their end is destruction, their god is the belly, and they glory in their shame, with minds set on earthly things (Phil 3:14ff.).

For the justice "in fair round belly" staring "with eyes severe", enter the judgment hall and observe Pontius Pilate. Complacency has slipped into his soul without raising the slightest alarm of his will; and that is not odd, because it has posed in fact as a form of eagerness, what Saint Benedict would call *zelus amaritudinis,* a zeal of bitterness that "separates from God and leads to hell" by thirsting deeply for shallow ends. If Pilate thirsted for anything, it was for the Emperor's approval; human respect, or dependence on what others think of oneself, knows no particular rank or class, but it is fatal to the perception of true justice and annihilates the integrity of the judge. Pilate may have seemed utterly detached from the Jews as he expressed contempt for their ways; he was in fact most solicitous of their favor when it might impress the Emperor as token of his administrative competence. Twice he had failed to prevent major riots among this ungovernable people, and he could not risk another. Pontius Pilate prayed fervently for the peace of Jerusalem, but for the love of Rome.

Here was complacency rampant, indifferent to truth and motivated by the opinions of others who are in a position to ensure the privilege of indifference. Thus in exasperation, Pilate asks "What is truth?" (Jn 18:38) and turns away before the Living Truth can reply. He oozed the vaunted bravado of the Roman imperium, but it was only apathy become a habit, the Stoic *ataraxy* expected of the well bred; today the advice is to "be cool", and it has in common with the old apathy at least a blithe aloofness to the claims of a truth beyond convenience. Thirst for justice is greatest when motivated by love as the ultimate measure of what is just; human respect, moral inertia, haughty conceit, are quick drinks by which the complacent please pride and concupiscence at the expense of justice. The fantastic nature of the apathetic moral construction may think that if 70 percent of the populace consider a crime to be just, then it is just; and in defiance, the justice of love cries out with parched lips, "If 70 percent of the people consider a crime to be justice, then 70 percent of the people are partners to a crime." Human complacency, however, is not impressed by divine logic; and the one reality about the complacent illusion is its power to pass itself off as real.

As the complacent have an intuition for spotting each other, they know how to entice, persuade, and impress each other with studied finesse. It is clearly seen at work in the events of Holy Week; the Passion of Christ was played out against the dispassion of the people. At the trial of Jesus, a most cynical dialogue between the Jews and Pilate set the undercurrent for the drama. Manipulators of the crowd knew exactly what to have them shout at the governor, the one threat that will quicken his "zeal of bitterness": "If you release him you are no friend of

Caesar . . . " (Jn 19:12). And Pilate was so conspicuously contemptuous of them that he was deaf to the corrosive contempt that these words betrayed. The complacent are so easily manipulated that they may actually think that they are in charge. With what seemed to him lofty swagger, Pilate refused to change the wording on the sign he had commissioned for the top of the cross; it was the minor triumph that satisfies those who think they are in control because they are in control of little things, and little things to them are all-important. Making sure he has the right to dictate the lettering on a sign takes his attention away from the awful letters being written in blood on the face of Heaven.

Power to Crucify the Truth

"Do you not know that I have power to release you and power to crucify you?" Pilate's fatuous boast of indifference to truth begs the inevitable answer of truth: "You would have no power over me unless it had been given to you from above . . . " (Jn 19:10–11). Pilate could have been a saint, as no one is born innately disqualified for holiness. If a marshal's baton was in the knapsack of every private in Napoleon's army, a cause for canonization is in every cradle of any nation. Pilate was no exception, nor was Judas, nor Julian the Apostate, nor Giles de Rais, nor the axe murderer on today's front page. Each might have been raised to the altars with a thousand candles, had they thirsted enough for the friendship of God. Instead, Pilate opts for the friendship of a petty local influence peddler, Herod Antipas, the tetrarch of Galilee, and in these darkening hours they seal their dark friendship. When complacent ambition forsakes justice out of human respect it simulates prudence on the middle way between vice and virtue. The court of Herod blushed on wine in amaranthine halls; and Pilate armored in the bronze of Rome was willing to giggle with them, just as the old brick Rome of Regulus would start silly songs on the marbled Palatine.

With irrevocable disdain at the thought of submitting to another's will, with the *Stolz* of the Germans and the *fierté* of the French and more than anything else the sneer of the Romans, Pilate affects condescension: he knows right from wrong but affects reluctance to impose his personal views on anyone else. But the rectitude even of the complacent is aware, and if it is not stirred when it is pricked, it is saddened. Some sultry breeze blows through the unventilated barracks of conscience. Dipping his hands in the ritual bowl of water, he proclaims his innocence of the blood of this just man. Christ must watch the drops of water that splash on the marble floor, the few drops some adjutant did not catch with a towel, and his cut lips thirst severely. Not for the water does he thirst; each drop is a symbol in his larger world of larger truths, and each is a soul. Christ thirsts for the soul of Pontius Pilate; if Pilate offers his heart he can live forever. Christ thirsts for the souls in the crowd; if they choose life instead of death they can live in a light that needs neither sun nor moon. He thirsts for the souls of the crowd. He thirsts for the souls of the nihilists who insinuate nothingness into the fullness of being; he thirsts for the souls of the materialists who say man is only bread, when he has said man does not live by bread alone; he thirsts for the souls of the collectivists who measure a man by the masses of men, when he has said that all are one in him.

So burdened with souls, the Bishop of Souls looks with wordless eyes at the Governor who claims power over him and his tears spell out: "You are in danger of going to hell!" It is the grammar of Love who thirsts in a world too drunk on itself to know the hurt of thirst. And how the complacent hypocrites profess scandal! It must be very hard for them to believe that anyone believes in hell. This man who has done no wrong knows what they cannot know: that there are souls beyond the great gulf of life and death who thirst for the one drop of water no one can give them; and they would not be so damned had they only in this life given one of the least of his little ones a cup of cold water in his name. Not in the name of guilt or sentiment or sanitary reform, but in the name of Christ who is in them. So deadly is apathy when it confronts the most majestic of Christ's solemn warnings, that it can only wonder what his real, that is, political, motive must be. "A man—a gentleman—ready to compromise would condemn Jesus to death again" (Ven. Josemaría Escrivá, *The Way*, no. 393).

The Crisis Resolved

In any soul's mid-life crisis, one may resolve to repair certain defects and inadequacies. One may promise to stop getting traffic tickets, to stop cheating on taxes, to stop smoking in national forests, to be more assiduous in advice to the children, to volunteer more time to worthy causes, and so on. But the sum total of reform legislation and telethons and ecological restoration is to no lasting avail without the counsel of Saint Augustine, who spoke of justice as love in the service of God alone. Justice is unjust if it does not thirst for God above all of God's creatures. Christ thirsts today as he thirsted on the cross, and though his objective triumph over sin and death has been won, he now appeals from the eminence of eternity for a moral triumph over the sin and death in each person made in his image.

Pascal, then, was teasing, but not touching, heresy when he said Christ is in agony until the end of the world; and in one perspective the agony is more mysterious in its divine intelligence, not a thirst wanting satisfaction but a satisfaction wanting a thirst. The initial grace, prevenient grace, is the supernatural awakening of the soul to a thirst, and when the soul recognizes God as its object, then the craving is acknowledged for the gift it is. It even becomes a motive for song. It would be foolish indeed to sing about being a camel that can do quite nicely without water, thank you very much; but the Psalmist was happy to start one of his anthems declaring that his soul was like a deer panting for the water brooks (Ps 42:1).

As selfish thirst, or complacency, is a "zeal of bitterness", this selfless thirst, or love, is a zeal of bliss. And in light of the inner perfection of the Holy Trinity it can be called a thirst only as an allegory of the divine awareness of creatures; in the economy of God's omnipotence, his awareness of anything is a summons to that thing to surrender to him. This is ground of freedom, and mere self-possession is relegated in spiritual fact to enslavement of the self, whether through a bourgeois deification of convention in the stead of God or through a bohemian deification of rejected convention. The smug sobriety of the complacent is as unworthy of the dignity of creatures as the divine thirst for souls is typical of a cosmic dignity "begotten, not made".

We who sin and die can presume to quench the thirst of Christ only by giving him sins repented and mortality regretted. As his thirst is morally a satisfaction waiting to

satisfy, human creatures serve his divine Majesty by finding satisfaction in him as the criterion for satisfaction in
anything else. Joy, then, is far more than a condition that
enters the human heart; it is the condition the human heart
enters when it longs for the justice of God. "Well done,
good and faithful servant; as you have been faithful over a
few things, I will make you ruler over many things; enter
into the joy of your Lord" (Mt 25:21). When this is believed,
and these words ring truer than any human promise,
human suffering finds its bliss on the cross, through and
not in spite of its pain. The venerable practice of "offering
up" pain and discomforts says it all quite simply; misap-
plied psychology may think that this is a way of sublimat-
ing a pain to a wishful ideal, when any saint knows that
suffering "offered up" realistically acknowledges the one-
sided divorce of earth from heaven, just as pleasure "offered
up" realizes the apocalyptic consummation of earth in
heaven. Christ's thirst for souls sacramentalizes marriage,
as a sign of the union between him and his redeemed
creation as the Church; but a divorce can never be a
sacrament, because that would be to bless unreality. Outside the Christian understanding of sin and death, then,
you have to consider suffering absurd, like the atheists, or
illusory like the Christian Scientists and other Dualists.
But then they have nothing to offer to Christ on the cross
for a thirst they do not think exists.

The peculiar concept of divine "jealousy", which so
exercises patrols on the lookout for anthropomorphic
crudities, makes all the sense in the world in these terms; it
means that the love of God is so great he will not permit a
bitter spirit of self-sufficiency, the false heroism of pride,
the driving engine of ambition and duplicity, to deny his
voluntary vulnerability. At least he will not permit it

without a fight, even death on a cross. And the so-called crisis of middle age is lifelong unless it is resolved by accepting a part in that drama and, by so doing, fracturing the dead hand of complacency on the human will.

The primitive and universal fact is illustrated in a story about the catechizing of the Frankish king Clovis before his baptism by Saint Remigius in 496. The pragmatic use he made of his new Christian status as an excuse for attacking the Arian Visigoths does not compromise his simplicity on the one point, the seriousness with which he approached the story of Christ. It only makes the gruff naïveté of the story all the more believable. The Salic Franks, one judges, were not an unjangled and quiet people or masters of understatement. On first hearing the account of the Passion, Clovis, then only a year or two short of the ideal thirty-three of Christ, grumbled: "If my army had been there, he'd never have been crucified!" Somewhat later, a second reading provoked a different observation: "If I had been there, I'd have stayed with his poor mother!" It is said that the bishop knew he was ready for the waters of baptism when the Passion was read again, and the king remarked without exclamation, "If I had been there, I'd have climbed up on the cross next to him."

CHAPTER SIX

DECLINE

"It is finished!"

COLOSSAL AND COMPLEX webs of critics have tried to find fault in Christ for two thousand years, some out of philosophical exasperation and some out of political desperation, some with great evil intent and some moved by a privately confected piety suspicious of foreign habits and impetuous instincts, and they have failed. At times they have done much harm to the Christian institution, or by inadvertence they have invigorated it by the very challenge, but the institution as they call it, that is, the Church, continues because they have never done harm to the Institutor. This cannot be said of any other historical figure.

When criticisms have limped, when arrows have broken against the perfection of his truth and the integrity of his person, the remnant recourse has been to say he was simply too good to be true, a self-projection of human desire. This, too, hits against the rock of reason: if he is a projection of our own heart's desire, how can he be too good to be true? If he is a sublimation of the highest tangible ideals, why is he unpredictable?

A self-projection can be read by the self, or it is not a self-projection. Why then did Jesus Christ seem such an illegible ambiguity, breaking men's hearts who could not read his? A broken hearted people thought the fulfillment of prophecy contradicted the prophets and blamed his tomb for seeming so cryptic.

"You did not choose me, but I chose you . . ." (Jn 15:16). This was his world before it was ours, and he knows it better than we do. God challenges Job out of the whirlwind: "Where were you when I laid the foundation of the earth?" (Job 38:4). He counsels through the prophet: "Before I formed you in the womb I knew you, and before you were born I consecrated you" (Jer 1:5). And from a mantle and heart of flesh, he declares before a sea of bewildered faces: "Before Abraham was, I am" (Jn 8:58). Those witnesses who had indeed rendered the promised Messiah a projection of themselves had contested him: "You are not yet fifty years old, and have you seen Abraham?" (Jn 8:57). But "I AM"is the agelessness of God and thus the identity of God to mortals. Being faithful to the laws as they understood them the Jews took up stones to safeguard the dignity of the I AM against this young carpenter of Nazareth who could have had a few grey hairs at most, and one or two wrinkles, but only where his eyes had squinted in the sun and where his mouth had laughed in the hidden places of his kingdom. Logic held hostage to itself can only cry: God is too big to fit in a man.

> In the year that King Uzziah died I saw the Lord sitting upon a throne high and lifted up; and his train filled the temple. . . . And I said: "Woe is me! For I am lost; for I am a man of unclean lips, and I dwell in the midst of a people of unclean lips; for my eyes have seen the King, the Lord of hosts!" (Is 6:1, 5).

You do not need a cosmology or a muddle of physics and theology to know that what Isaiah saw was bigger than the universe. Information like that is revealed to the interior eye; human vision is by its nature myopic when unassisted from without. Had you asked any passerby at the time of our Lord who the greatest man was, the common choice hands down would have been Tiberius. He would have said otherwise. Tiberius was weary of what greatness offered, at least in its concrete aspects. The pomp of Rome was so much noise, and its tenements and temples one vast and unpleasant hive to him; but he was not completely mad, so he retired to Capri. There in the slow procession of days he could watch the sky and sea lying against each other and feed pet goldfish in cobalt pools and lick honey from his fingertips under a honey sun. All oblivious to a carpenter from Nazareth hanging on a cross. But if anyone had startled the Emperor out of his balmy reverie just to say a man who claimed to be king had been executed on the other side of the other sea, he would have shrugged and dipped his fingers back in the honey pot: "That cut him down to size."

A Measure of Empires

One problem with empires is that they trace the world on such a scale that the scale itself becomes tiresome; and cultural sophistication and political dominance breed a certain moral fatigue and even apprehension. No one ever suffers from air-weariness or light-weariness or gravity-weariness, because air and light and gravity are in due proportion by their nature, but when we expand our influence and impressions beyond the scope of useful synthesis, a peculiar condition known as world-weariness sets in. "Dominion over palm and pine" breeds a wistful desire for hamlets and hearths, and even empresses may withdraw to some gaslit corner of the castle to darn socks and sing "Home, Sweet Home".

And by the same token, when the image of God in a

soul appears too large for the ego's capacity to understand,
it is easier to sentimentalize its quaintness by cutting the
image down to size. From the noon hour on Good Friday
we have seen the efficient role that sentimentalists play in
crucifying. As cynicism attends disappointed political
ambition, so a certain sentimental defensiveness accompanies
disappointed spiritual expectations. It happens with a thud
when those expectations have been human projections.
Solemn speeches begin to sound like cant, and triumphal
ceremonies suddenly hang loose and "triumphalistic" on
the bony shoulders of a civilization that wonders if it
might just withdraw from mighty thoughts and diction
altogether.

The gravest of dangers confronts a weary culture when
it begins to suspect that the Living Elders are senilities too
old to think, and that all the saints are like the unctuous
cardinal who hid a lobster salad side, and that Catholicism
itself might be a great idea somewhat overplayed.

When the ages of man slowly pass their days of confidence, like empires they enter a sunset, left with a few
bugles and plumes.

> The sixth age shifts
> Into the lean and slipper'd pantaloon,
> With spectacles on nose, and pouch on side;
> His youthful hose well sav'd, a world too wide
> For his shrunk shank; and his big manly voice,
> Turning again toward childish treble, pipes
> And whistles in his sound.

When Jesus was twelve years old, he found doctors of
religion like that in the temple. Men dim-sighted from
years of poring over the holy scrolls, prayer shawls hanging limp on shrinking frames, voices bereft of old timbre

and slightly cracking like the changing voice of the boy,
declared this day a man, who speaks to them. To the
patient and reverent old men the temple was getting larger
and more mysterious as daily they found new portents in
the written words of the God whose house it was. Not so
the youngest man, the oldest boy, who stared at them; he
had already shown an unsettling familiarity with the holy
temple, drawn back to it as though to a magnet, roaming
confidently through its precincts like someone sent to
check how tenants are managing a familiar old property.
"But those tenants said among themselves, 'This is the heir;
come let us kill him, and the inheritance will be ours.' And
they took him and killed him, and cast him out of the
vineyard" (Mk 12:7–8).

The temple passageways and colonnades are of a plan
known to him in a way he could not have absorbed from
his infant's glance when he had been carried there with a
couple of turtledoves a dozen years before. A blueprint is
in his mind, as vivid as the predictable charts of the sky
sold by the astrologers in dusty corners of the city. He
stares at the curtain before the Holy of Holies where he is
not allowed, and he knows its secret without having to go
in. He prays before the closed curtain, head bowed and
arms outstretched like the others; only if you listened
carefully could you notice that when the others say "our
Father" he says "my Father". When the rabbis speak in
whistling voices, he questions them no longer boyishly
but rather trumpeting. All of which astonishes the rabbis,
of course, and perhaps even rattles their agreeably lugubri-
ous nostalgia; but more astonishing is his reply to the
domestic confrontation when he is found at last.

Mary would reprimand him, though there never is
found sharpness in her rebukes; their exchanges, both of

the most human sort and freighted with curt explosions of mysterious dogma, always seem smiled as much as spoken. Her intellect, and properly so, is not as informed as her will, and she complains with matriarchal propriety about his dallying, as though he had been lost, at the nervous expense of others. In ordinary stories at this point, a twelve-year-old religious genius would have said something ghastly edifying, like the fellow George Eliot described as "always making you a present of his opinions". Instead, the "lost" boy who had come from eternity to find a lost world replies without a hint of priggishness or brattishness, but timelessly: "How is it that you sought me? Did you not know that I must be in my Father's house?" (Lk 2:49).

Even the temple is not home to him who will have no place on earth to lay his head save a cross; his home is higher, and this temple is a place for work on the way home. The temple is a tabernacle, a petrified tent, but still a tent, as a silent symbol for Divine Presence who is more transitory than foxes who at least have holes and birds who at least have nests. "But when Christ appeared as a high priest of the good things that have come, then through the greater and more perfect tent (not made with hands, that is, not of this creation), he entered once for all into the holy Place, taking not the blood of goats and calves but his own blood, thus securing an eternal redemption" (Heb 9:11–12). And pity the man who does try to confine God to the dimensions of the earthly temple.

The Blessed Lady and Joseph happily do not try to domesticate the remoter ways of this son; theirs is a stewardship over him and not a colonizing power. Their entire ambition and promise was to be fit enough to accommodate their Lord and God. By lives of heroic humility, then, and by nothing else since they had nothing else of consequence, they were able to make their hovel in Nazareth a place fit for a king.

Sin is an inappropriate urge to colonize God's creation, to be kings of it instead of tenants, to kill the heir and declare an imperium of the ego. It happens in myriad ways, causing an avalanche of social enormities and public neglects of the commonweal; but it happens immediately and most radically in the life of worship, when men claim proprietary rights over the House of God; and when it is achieved, a dreadful weariness of the spirit sets in, unsure of itself, ridiculing its own triumphalism and replacing high Catholic liturgy with *gemütlich* para-liturgy. And sometime soon it will dawn on us like a clap of summer thunder that all the contrived folksiness around the altar, the running commentaries and self-conscious informality and lazy postures and neglect of noble art, have been the gauche opposite of humility: the intrusion of the personality into the ageless rites is human pride unwilling to be smaller than God. And should any hapless priest or prelate want to tell a joke or two during the course of the sacred rites, let him confine himself to the witticisms that passed between Our Lady and John as Christ was dying on the cross above. If he can find them.

When Isaiah saw God he cried in splendid awe; it is not always the reaction one gets upon entering a church. It can hardly be so if the Real Presence of Christ has been shunted off to a poor waiting room, or if we pad in on wall-to-wall carpeting where all is soft and indirect, including the preaching and hymns. It often seems now, as then, in our promiscuity with transcendence that he came to his own people, and his own people tried to housebreak him. This was the willful domestication of the Incarnation that Mary and Joseph refused to attempt. And the priest who is not prostrate before the altar of Christ the King as a living transparency of the divine Fatherhood he mediates will brood high and lifted up from his own chair, "presiding" over a decaying empire that defines itself anemically as a "faith community". Reluctance to say, "Woe is me!" is audacity to say "Look at me", and at the end of the decay one will be left staring at oneself.

Right doctrine is not enough to put insufferable smugness out of its own misery. Orthodoxy is not enough. These are evidences of grace, but grace itself lives in holiness. Only holiness can be at peace with God in his temple without lapsing into nostalgia or contempt. Renewal of the soul means that people accustomed to doing things to God begin to let God do things to them, initiating changes in their eccentricities, vices, and habits. The one way to avoid being passive about the Passion is to be passive before it, vulnerable to the grace it secures for the soul. This is the disposition of heart that the Lord requires, as from the cross the eternal Bridegroom of creation asks, "Friend, how did you get in here without a wedding garment?" (Mt 22:12). Any other disposition is a psychological cosmetic. To an age whose epidemic response to the aging process is to go out and get a face-lift, the eucharistic bidding is, "Lift up your hearts."

Christ is lifted up on the cross to begin this "Sursum corda". It is the fearsome carpentry his Father sent him into the world to do. And much as he loved the temple, to the extent of commanding those he healed to submit themselves to its priests, he had not come to restore it or even to purify it. Redemption is too radical to be a restoration, and the consequent measure of sanctity will not be the degree to which orthodox belief is restored. The restoration of Catholicism does not consist of reassembling

a past golden age; it is nothing if it is not the reassembling of the Body of Christ in its oneness, holiness, cath-
olicity, and apostolicity. When Christ wept over Jerusalem,
he was not showing upset at its bad drainage or vulgar
imperial additions; not until the Last Day will his whole
distress be understood, but his burden involves us. The
Redeemer's business is very different from repairing the
temple as though he were gentrifying some dilapidated
brownstone; and our business is not to reclaim a fourth or
twelfth or sixteenth century, gasping "Look, Teacher, what
wonderful stones and what wonderful buildings!" (Mk
13:1). Swearing by some past golden age is like swearing
by the gold on the altar; it is forbidden by Christ who is
the living altar and accepts no offering before he accepts
hearts. The rich young man of the parable learned this to
his sorrow; our century has learned this to its neurotic
sorrow, and the imperial age of the ego turned away from
its Master and walked into the sunset like the man who
went away grieved for the strangest of reasons, "for he had
great possessions" (Mk 10:22).

Each soul is a unique thought of God, and only when
the soul submits to the divine will does the Holy Spirit
think that thought in it. Otherwise, the soul shrinks and
whistles like a collapsing pipe organ leaking sounds of
what one might have been. The most radical repudiation
of humanity is the reluctance to be a saint; it is more
regrettable than the tonnage of collapsed empires and
crumbling economic systems, because Christ is crucified
for souls, and to reject the call to holiness is to reject the
architecture of freedom that he finishes on the cross. The
key is for grace to make the free will desire freedom above
willfulness; this is the functional equivalent of crucifying
the self, since freedom receives its permission from the
same will of God that wills the cross.

As human freedom is created, it does not compromise itself by "being crucified with Christ", that is, with conforming to the love of God; it becomes not only freedom but free precisely by becoming the function of the unoriginate will of God planted within it by grace. "But by the grace of God I am what I am, and his grace toward me was not in vain" (I Cor 15:10). Passivity of the soul to the divine will is thus a very active and vital passion, because God wills that the human will should act. And still, the human will is not human if it is not free, and it is not free if it is confined to itself. "It's a free country and I'll do what I want", surrenders the self to the self in a most demeaning way.

Paradoxically, we are not freely human until our wills are deified, and we are not deified without ceasing to idolize the self. The freedom of holiness, or salvation, is totally dependent on God and on the self simultaneously. Here, to the refutation of Quietists and some "born again" pietists, is the necessary collaboration of the human will and God's gratuitous action. " ... work out your own salvation with fear and trembling; for God is at work in you, both to will and to work, for his good pleasure" (Phil 2:12–13). Its paradoxical aspect is due to the inadequacy of human language that has no schematic grammar for the coexistence of Being and being; but it is no problem for heavenly language, which has no need of grammar. Suffice it to say that when Christ was a carpenter human and divine, the divine knew what he must do, and the human needed to have the wood in front of him to do it. A log in Jerusalem was of no use to the carpenter in Nazareth; and so with souls, who may have their thoughts in many places, while the Master requires the accessibility of their intellects and wills in order to accomplish his Father's business. "Martha, Martha, you are anxious and troubled about many things; one thing is needful. Mary has chosen the good portion, which shall not be taken away from her" (Lk 10:41–42).

The World Cut down to Size

The laws of metaphysics are deeper than physics, but they are not concealed from human reason. They are laws, after all, and the intellect calls them so. There is nothing in the mind by its own nature, then, that makes it impossible to conceive of the coming of the Creator into his creation. An Idealist may wrongly think that if something is in the mind it is in fact, but that has nothing to do with Christian revelation. Christianity insists that if a thing is in fact then it is available to the mind, provided the mind is a factory and not a dormitory: we may imagine vainly, but the vainest thing is not to imagine at all, and the difference lies in the use of the material insights and evidences at our disposal. "O foolish men, and slow of heart to believe all that the prophets have spoken!" (Lk 24:26).

If in the regimen of physics a painter cannot enter the landscape on his canvas, this is no intrinsic impediment to a deeper power of the Word who "utters" people and lands and imaginations into being, to become flesh and dwell among us. Nor can so fragile a being as the human call impossible a Trinity of love so infinitely free that this freedom spins itself outside of itself to create a universe of planets and dusts, glaciers and deserts, elephants and fleas. The divine love made the human person, and the uniqueness of the person is not an isolation of the person. We are not alone, and that is so because we are creatures in a creation.

But we are also not meant to be alone, and that is so because we are creatures of the Holy Trinity. Personhood may be the most conspicuous human fact; it is also the most mysterious human fact (the deepest mysteries are always the most conspicuous): it reflects the supernatural life of the Trinitarian Persons. " . . . the Church possesses, thanks to the Gospel, the truth about man. This includes an anthropology which the Church does not cease to fathom and communicate. The primordial affirmation of this anthropology is that of man as the image of God, irreducib e to a simple parcel of nature, or as an anonymous element of the human community" (John Paul II: Discourse in Mexico, January 28, 1979).

Complacency makes a habit of denying that, if only because it taxes the mind too much. But such a flagrant form of world-weariness is a contradiction of the creatureliness of the human spirit. If you drop enough pride into it, the alchemy produces anxiety, the spiritual malaise of unmortified wills that cloaks itself in the splendor of God's creation and calls it a shroud.

> Therefore I tell you, do not be anxious about your life, what you shall eat or what you shall drink, nor about your body, what you shall put on. Is not life more than food, and the body more than clothing? Look at the birds of the air: they neither sow nor reap nor gather into barns, and yet your heavenly Father feeds them. Are you not of more value than they? And which of you by being anxious can add one cubit to his span of life? (Mt 6:25–27; cf. Lk 12:22ff.).

God feeds and clothes the human body with great truths, and when they hang so limp on bare-boned pride, it is easier to cut them down. The biggest words, transub-

stantiation and infallibility and sanctifying grace are quickly
sheared down to memorials and opinions and kindliness.
When the embodiment of all these great realities was taken
before the Sanhedrin, the supreme council of the Jews, the
high priest Caiaphas adjured him "by the living God, tell
us if you are the Christ, the Son of God". "You have said
so. But I tell you, hereafter you will see the Son of man
seated at the right hand of power, and coming on the
clouds of heaven" (Mt 26:63–64). Caiaphas tears his lovingly
woven robes: "Blasphemy!" As an attempt to co-opt the
cosmic drama, it is as comic as it is tragic: there was a ritual
for tearing these robes along a special seam, like a perfo-
rated package, so that the cloth would not be ruined. So
even wild wrath had its codes, and indignation could be
recycled. When life is played out on so small a stage and
under such tidy constraints, violence is on the miniature
scale of dyspepsia: "I am shocked!" Then back to the
keyboard, or whatever.

Notice how, when God's own faithful grow weary and
shrunken by familiarity with holy things, they begin to
accuse God himself of irreverence. It happens subtly and
even unconsciously, but with great consistency: Chrysostom
encountered it in Constantinople and so did Ambrose in
Milan when they spoke the plain truth against allegorizers
and self-justifiers. But the daily news makes such archeol-
ogy unnecessary: we have had ample cases in recent times
of cathedrals in the United States invaded and desecrated
by champions of perverse causes, fanatics accusing God
himself of corrupting his creation through the persistent
moral demands of his Church. This may mark the last gasp
of modern foolishness or the first cry of a birthing barbarism;
but ours is not the first age to have such conflicting forces.
Seven and a half centuries ago Pope Gregory IX wrote

quite matter-of-factly that "the evening of the world is declining", and he might well have pointed to the death of his friend Francis of Assisi and the survival of the tempestuous Emperor Frederick II. So as the sun continued to shine, it is useless to anticipate the judgment of time on the times; but that notwithstanding, a lesson of the fractious spirit of our own time is the futility of the human tendency to fear that its ego might be desecrated by holiness.

Christ had to defend his Father's rights over the Temple: "I tell you, something greater than the temple is here. And if you had known what this means, 'I desire mercy and not sacrifice', you would not have condemned the guiltless. For the Son of man is lord of the Sabbath" (Mt 12:8). That which has been called modernity perpetuates a very old assault against the primacy of God in history; and it is never so archaic as in its readiness to accuse God of acting beneath himself when he asserts his rights over material being. Modernity has been many things, but as much as anything it has been institutionalized subjectivism scandalized by the intervention of God. When the modern response to spiritual promptings has been to revive pagan forms, through racial and economic and nature myths for instances, divinity has been kept well away from morals; a Nazi can worship his blood stock, a Marxist his class, a Liberal progress, and each one in so doing is united oddly enough in denying any transcendent significance to private moral behavior. The total ideological myth does not expect high things of the soul; it has abandoned the contingent soul for the myth of soullessness.

In his *True Humanism,* Maritain pinpointed the fiction of ideology in its portrayal of history as an "automatism of essences" rather than a progression of existential contingencies. God, "the free head of free agents", would be unnecessary, not even a polite convention, in a cultural platonism of pure essences. And when the Church invokes the name of God, refusing to rescind or alter the apostolic affidavits and existential truths of the Faith, the ideologues, be they at the moment people with mythically progressive views on children or sexuality or economic justice or what have you, indignantly array themselves before the camera spotlights to cry: "Blasphemy!" as did once a crowd to the Son of God himself under a glowering sky.

The Father's Business

Some Soviet citizens have launched a campaign to reconstruct a cathedral in Moscow. Unpredictable realignments and conversions are shaping the map of Christian practice. Suddenly, theology stands more erect than those sciences that from time to time were tempted to replace it; since the fall of the Berlin Wall, said one editor, roughly 90 percent of all standard political science texts have become useless, and this cannot be said of the Gospel. Whether cathedrals survive in the West and rise anew in the East, churches are being recovered or restored in many parts of the former Communist empire at the same time that they are being desecrated by insulters or denuded and neglected by the lukewarm in places long thought free. "The men of Nineveh will arise at the judgment with this generation and condemn it; for they repented at the preaching of Jonah, and behold, something greater than Jonah is here" (Lk 11:32). A new astonishment is attaching itself to the promise that "neither on this mountain nor in Jerusalem" will we worship the Father for "the hour is coming, and now is, when the true worshippers will worship the Father in spirit and truth, for such the Father seeks to worship him" (Jn 4:21, 23).

Christ bleeds on the cross as the work his Father has given him; the theological doctrine of covenant is a surprisingly, even shockingly, graphic business contract to die for the people. It is only because Christ "emptied himself, taking the form of a servant, being born in the likeness of men" (Phil 2:7), that faith dares to speak of the matter in pragmatic terms without being absurd.

> Therefore, brethren, since we have confidence to enter the sanctuary by the blood of Jesus, by the new and living way which he opened for us through the curtain, that is, through his flesh, and since we have a great priest over the house of God, let us draw near with a true heart in full assurance of faith, with our hearts sprinkled clean from an evil conscience and our bodies washed with pure water (Heb 10:19–22).

There is, and not as a figure of speech, a world of difference between ending and finishing; and the surest guarantee against fading out like the "lean and slipper'd pantaloon" is to know the difference. Christ has a work to finish, and it is the work that he began when the world began, the creation of a delight capable of perfectly reciprocating the love that made it. If the whole prospect seems daunting, and if modern spiritual capacity has at times been too shriveled to be anything but intimidated by it and hardened by its threat, the only solution is an affirmation that shakes dormant energies: Christ himself is the curtain through which the littleness of temporality has access to the wideness of eternity, welcoming existential survival into the life of grace not so much by insinuation as by a loud slap of reality.

> Thus it is written, that the Christ should suffer and on the third day rise from the dead, and that repentance and

forgiveness of sins should be preached in his name to all
nations, beginning from Jerusalem. You are witness of
these things. And behold, I send the promise of my
father upon you; but stay in the city, until you are
clothed with power from on high (Lk 24:46–49).

At the age of twelve he was intent on doing it, and
the power of his presence was remarked by the frail rabbis in tassels grown too big for them; and when the
grown man was brought handcuffed into the same precincts,
the greatest of the elders shook their tassels indignantly
at the same invading power. At twelve it seemed precocious, and the elders whistled their amused wonder; at
thirty-three it was outright defiance of the laws and manners
with which human pride digs and hedges its garden, and
he is slapped. And nothing changes the confidence of
his purpose: "If I have spoken wrongly, bear witness to
the wrong, but if I have spoken rightly, why do you strike
me?" (Jn 18:23).

In the declining years of Israel, the Messianic promise
became louder until it was written and sealed in blood.
"For where a will is involved, the death of the one who
made it must be established. For a will takes effect only at
death, since it is not in force as long as the one who made
it is alive" (Heb 9:16–17). Now why God ordained it that
way is known to God, and those of us on the receiving end
have the rational obligation to acknowledge it when it
happens. The blood runs down the cross, down the little
rock that reminded morbid imaginations of a skull, down
through the streets of Jerusalem mostly filled with people
indifferent to the crimson tide, down through the dynas-
ties and epochs that have either spilled the blood on themselves or drunk it in ruby chalices, down through the
streets of our own cities whose morose burdens are his,

and onto the waiting altars of the Church for which he died. That is what Christ came into this world to accomplish.

Whether we believe it or not, it happened. Should the garments of faith outsize the frames of shrunken perception, and should the treble voices of faith be too wizened to sing the depths of praise, it happened. When the blood was poured out, he looked at a world shriveled in the ancient robes that had been spun for her from the looms of heaven. Then, it was then according to those who heard it, creation's last young voice shouted: "It is finished!"

CHAPTER SEVEN

OLD AGE

"Father, into thy hands I commend my spirit!"

The Discoverable Self

HUMAN INTELLIGENCE makes three discoveries basic to the integrity of life. The primary is physical: in the first two years of existence, a baby receives most of the neurological information needed to live a lifetime, discovering "What I am". The second discovery is psychological, attained through the various critical confrontations in childhood and adolescence and in fact never ending: the fact of personality is confronted by sorting through the economy of passions and appetites, the structures of individuality that limit and transfigure the person, discovering "Who I am". Thirdly is the spiritual revelation of purpose, resolving to the soul's great peace or distraction the motivation and end by which existence is transformed into the completeness of being described as fullness of joy (Jn 15:11; 16:24; 17:13; 1 Jn 1:4; 2:12), discovering what it means to be born and live and die, or "Why I am".

Carnal mindedness, though it may seem fully grown and mature, never quite passes beyond the first preoccupation with the body. When it professes to be a new form of liberation, it accidentally advertises its arrested emotional development and perpetually infantile judgment, repeatedly asking as an apostrophe with no possibility of objective answer, "What am I?"

Then there is the habitual neurosis, possibly prosperous and even opulent in the material order and reconciled to minor gratifications and amusements, whose definition is an irresolution of the question in the second dimension: "Who am I?"

Finally is the movement on inquiry past immaturity and neurosis into plain and simple sloth. Here is the murky state in which an otherwise formed intelligence cuts a detour around the definitive challenge to itself: "Why am I alive? Who made me? What will become of me?" Either the central question is not raised, or it is raised and quickly dropped. The "What" is answerable, and so is the "How?", but the slothful mind lacks the heart, and the slothful heart lacks the mind for confronting the "Why".

When Christ comes to earth from heaven, he lets us discover him in three ways, too, but in an order reversing the approach from earth to heaven. As we learn from an earthly perspective first biologically, then psychologically, and then spiritually, he teaches the spiritual mystery of God first. "All things have been delivered to me by my Father; and no one knows the Son except the Father, and no one knows the Father except the Son and any one to whom the Son chooses to reveal him" (Mt 11:27; cf. Jn 3:34–35). This is what he does when he opens the scroll in the synagogue of Nazareth: "Today this scripture has been fulfilled in your hearing" (Lk 4:21). And when he teaches in parables along the way: "This is why I speak to them in parables, because seeing they do not see, and hearing they do not hear, nor do they understand" (Mt 13:13). And when he preaches in full view: "Seeing the crowds, he went up on the mountain . . . " (Mt 5:1; cf. Mk 3:13; Jn 6:3).

In withdrawn encounters, he introduces the select company of his disciples to the mystery of his person. "To you it has been given to know the secrets of the kingdom of Heaven, but to them it has not been given" (Mt 13:11; Mk 4:11; cf. 1 Cor 5:12–13). The question, "Who am I?", is answered in private interrogations on the coastland: "For flesh and blood has not revealed this to you, but my Father who is in heaven" (Mt 16:17). And when he pours forth a new light on the mountaintop: "But Jesus came and touched them, saying, 'Rise, and have no fear'" (Mt 17:7). And in some corner after a dinner: "For you will always have the poor with you, but you will not always have me" (Mt 26:11).

Reserved for last is the meaning of his flesh; that which is the elementary fact of fallen man is the most disorienting fact of the Perfect Man. The most attractive heresies of the Faith, as a matter of history, have tried to settle the mystery of Eternity Enfleshed by banishing the discovery as a mirage. Mere materialism, as it tarnishes, lives unwilling to accept the freedom of which God is the effective cause; it does not invalidate the gigantic principle of holy materialism, the sacramentality of created things, and the sacredness of the flesh. When religions of the perfumed and illiterate temples or arid and pedantic meeting houses examined the body, they commonly and instinctively either did it with a leer or with a sneer; cult prostitution and sectarian prudery got the flesh wrong because the very idea of a sacrament was absurd to both. To one the Living Word was unutterable and to the other the Living Bread was unspeakable. And matters were not helped by a modern revival of pagan crudeness more childish than childlike, more vulgar than primitive. Instance cults like Mormonism and the Jehovah's Witnesses that reduce divinity exclusively to materiality: this is the nursery notion that for all time God has been material, that the Word believed by Christians to have been made flesh simply is flesh.

Diverse as they are in expression and representation, the manifold confusions spring from attempts to be logical outside God's historical categories, and all of them dash into frail spray on the gigantic rocks of Christian materialism: "Do you not know that your body is a temple of the Holy Spirit within you, which you have from God? You are not your own; you were bought with a price. So glorify God in your body" (1 Cor 6:19–20). It is too great a wonder not to be kept until the end. Left to the garish noon of Good Friday is the discovery of what he is, but not until it is intimated in the lamplight of a rented room the night before:

> Now as they were eating, Jesus took bread, and blessed, and broke it, and gave it to his disciples and said, "Take, eat; this is my body." And he took a cup, and when he had given thanks he gave it to them saying, "Drink of it, all of you; for this is my blood of the covenant, which is poured out for many for the forgiveness of sins" (Mt 26:26–28; Mk 14:22–25; Lk 22:17–19).

Exposed and isolated on the cross is the biological fact of what it costs the divine humility to ransom many. Those who in frustration had called him a devil can see the quivering flesh of a man, and those who in panic had mistaken him for a ghost can see the red blood of a man.

Reverence shown to Christ's body when it was removed from the cross was a tradition of Jewish burial customs, but the good graveside etiquette of anointing the remains was totally transformed by the fact that this body belonged to the Son of Man: " . . . we firmly believe that when his soul was dissociated from his body, his divinity continued always united both to his body in the sepulchre and to his soul in limbo" (Catechism of the Council of Trent, I. 5.6). The Church's devotion to the Precious Blood is thus pitched on a high evangelical note, not shrill or maudlin but

sonorous, as that struck by Pope John XXIII in 1962:
"...the infinite love of the Savior is announced in his
Name, symbolized in his Heart, and made eloquent in his
Blood." The I AM who needs no definition, by an act of
ineffable love submits himself to exposing a purpose for
his coming to man, and an identity, yet in nothing is his
condescension more mysterious than when he subjects his
human nature as a human spectacle. The Why of the I AM
and the Who of the I AM are preludes to What the I AM
makes himself for us. By abasement of innocent flesh, he
opens guilty flesh to an imperishable future all within the
context of real life rightly ordered in the material realm,
and the violence it does to long-settled religious disposi-
tions is so great that the mightiest religious systems will
call him a blasphemer in Jerusalem and cannibal king in
Rome, scandalous in the synagogue and foolish in the
academy, the antithesis of religion and the fomenter of
irreligion and ruin.

> So it is with the resurrection of the dead. What is sown is
> perishable, what is raised is imperishable. It is sown in
> dishonor, it is raised in glory. It is sown in weakness, it is
> raised in power. It is sown a physical body, it is raised a
> spiritual body. If there is a physical body, there is also a
> spiritual body. Thus it is written, "The first man Adam
> became a living being"; the last Adam became a life-
> giving spirit. But it is not the spiritual which is first but
> the physical, and then the spiritual. (1 Cor 15:42–46).

Religion and Body Language

The wood of the cross does speak, whenever conscience
listens, and its message is as plain as it is hard: schizophre-
nia about the life of the soul is as pathological as schizo-

phrenia about anything else. "Religion" has a double root; probably the original one means to read over again, to examine and take seriously, while the other root refers to binding or taking on an obligation; but taken as a whole, religion is taking seriously the most serious things, and that cannot mean picking and choosing, or prefabricating fundamentals. Being a serious obligation to the truth, religion cannot be about itself without being flippant or independent: "It doesn't matter what you believe as long as you believe in something." Because truth is true, there can only be right and wrong beliefs. And the easiest way to avoid the serious obligation to truth is to become aesthetical about it.

Aestheticism as its own industry is to beauty what mere religiosity is to religion: not serious about obligations and not obliged to seriousness. As mere aestheticism is the rather inflated and fuzzy concept of art for art's sake, religiosity is religion for the sake of religion, and it is schizophrenic because it contradicts itself by wanting to be about itself. It can happen in any institution neglectful of its purpose: bureaucracy is government without governing, clerisy is sacrifice without sacrificing, profligacy is pleasure without pleasing. Aestheticism and religiosity attract each other by their mutual absentmindedness about their ends: aestheticism is the pursuit of beauty to an ugly degree, and religiosity is the practice of religion to the point of irreligion.

Aestheticism has been positively thrilled by artistic trends whose chief justification has been a quality of shocking or repulsing the uninitiated; and religiosity has physically built church councils and vast edifices without much serious belief in the physical resurrection of Christ. Rather predictably, then, religiosity becomes aesthetical about the cross, wearing it instead of hanging on it. The early Christians could not be that way, because Calvary was too close, and they knew the difference between pierced hands and pierced ears.

The intensity with which the Passion of Christ mixes physicality and spirituality annihilates merely superficial attempts to appropriate it. When the Sacrifice of Calvary is offered in the Holy Eucharist, aestheticism may look elsewhere for inspiration until it finds a spiritual wilderness called a "high". Religiosity will turn to creatures to supplant the uncreated holiness of the Mass, until spiritual freedom is enslaved to particular ethnic customs or charismatic spokesmen. Those biases against the authentic drama of the cross always blame something other than themselves for their failure. The Mass is too long, for instance. A holy priest had a holy answer: " 'The Mass is long', you say, and I reply, 'Because your love is short'."

The human will is moved to love the divinity of Christ in awareness of the divine assumption of humanity. And thus Christianity is far from the self-projection that some psychologists have called it, and it is an almost entirely reflexive response to a divine injection into the realm of human perception. Christ inserts himself into time and space, insinuates himself into speech, and inscribes himself into history to the astonishment of each who encounters him: "How do you know me?" (Jn 1:48). He reorders the pagan process of making biology theology by making theology biology, ending the shadowy and cryptic tendency of man to bow down to wooden gods and supplanting it with a decision of God to be bowed down on wood. "If I have told you earthly things and you do not believe, how can you believe if I tell you heavenly things? No one has ascended into heaven but he who descended from heaven, the Son of man" (Jn 3:12–13).

From this injection of eternity into human experience, or the theological "scandal of particularity", human speculation is informed of its limits; the barest tremor of a wrist whose nerves have been ripped by a nail banishes each comforting but pointless impression of religion as abstraction. The Crucified One is not an abstraction, and he is not crucified for abstractions. Sickness is an abstraction, and he never did eradicate sickness; the sick are not abstractions, and he manifestly did heal them. Hunger is an abstraction, and to the confusion of many social philosophers he did not eliminate it; the hungry are solid if empty, and he filled them with good things. He blesses the meek, not meekness; and he blesses the humble while knowing that humility will be cursed by the proud until the end of the world.

A daring man might call Christianity the least spiritual of all religions and be called a blasphemer by religionists and a vulgarian by aesthetes, as Christ was insulted by Herodians and Sadducees alike. Again, as Maritain explained true humanity:

> An ideological policy, be it jacobin or clerical, knows only pure essences (duly simplified), and we can have a firm confidence that ... platonism will always lead, with an infallible rectitude, to non-existence. In history ... it is not theses that confront one another, neatly set out on the pages of a book, or as in some academic discussion ... it is concrete forces charged with humanity, heavy with their weight of fatalities and contingencies. ...

Christianity is the manifestly complete and pragmatic resolution of the spiritual drama, and at the same time is the least spiritual of all religions because it is not a religion. That is to say, it is not a factor of thinking and living that can be compartmentalized as one item among others, like "Religion" in a weekly magazine given its page along with sections on "World Events" and "The Economy" and "Sports". If religion is something "done" on one day of the week, the religionist will quickly be undone by it, the unity of his life destroyed by the notion of it as the complexity of parts among which moral uplift is one prominent consideration. To "sell what you possess" (Mt 19:21) can mean one thing if the speaker is your stock broker, and something else if he is your lawyer; but when he is the Lord of the Universe, it means to get rid of the notion of him as the founder of a religion and his followers as religious. Religions show the way through mystery; Christianity is the mystery because it is Christ. It would be edifying to put on a theory called Christianity; but instead, the Apostle says to put on Christ. It makes all the difference between being edified and being sanctified; and if this keeps getting in the way of eclectic religiosity, it is by the very nature of Christ who is "The Way". Among "the world's great religions" Christianity is the most subversive, because its whole point is that the meaning of the world and the meaning of greatness are to be found in the end of religion. On this point, Christianity is far more similar to atheism than to religions. The crucial difference is that atheism is unreal: it says the crucial difference hangs on an idea, and Christianity says it hangs on a cross.

The Problem of Self-Projection

By the uncompromising force of this claim come the seriousness and obligation of Christianity above any religious system; the imitation of Christ is unlike the imitation of any religious figure. Copies are counterfeit unless they are stamped with the original, and authentic Christianity does not originate in a Christ who is but a hero. Christ is the Savior in a cosmic and supernatural dimension, and unless he is accepted as such he is larger than life, that melodramatic hero who lives above the human condition of the Christ who lives through it. Popular heroes exaggerate the body, but Christ makes his body be a body.

There are four basic types of heroism. The strong silent type represents impassibility, as the theologians speak of it in reference to the serenity of God himself. But the crucifixion makes Christ cry in pain. The superman type represents subtlety, the ability of God to penetrate and conquer material obstacles: " . . . the body is totally subject to the soul and ever ready to obey its wishes" (Catechism of the Council of Trent, I. 12.13). But on the cross Christ is the victim of wood and nails. The celebrity type represents clarity, a conspicuous radiance of form set apart from mortals by the attention of spotlights. But instead of a spotlight, Christ is crucified under a darkening and obscuring sky. The fourth heroic type represents the explorer, widely traveled and informed of exotic ways, the jet-setter. But Christ is immobile on the cross, pinned like a mounted moth.

Yet when Christ rises from the dead he will exhibit all four heroic characters, refuting comparisons with extraordinary figures born of our own world and wills, individuals who oblige one or another type. In the resurrection, Christ will be impassible (he suffers no more and shows the prints in his body as emblems of triumph); he will become history's authentic case of subtlety as he appears in the Upper Room, the doors being shut in fear; clarity will be his silent witness from the first dawnlight on Easter morning to the firelight on the Galilean shore to the radiance of an open heaven whose "lamp is the Lamb" (Rev 21:23). And as for agility, his will and not distance will govern his appearances to a few here and many there in those forty days when he did things that all the world's books could not contain (cf. Jn 21:25). Christ becomes all types of hero because, as Christianity is not a religion so much as it is the fulfillment of religion, so the Christ of Christianity is not a hero in any way so much as he is the fulfillment of heroism, the summation of the protoheroic types.

None of this qualifies or compromises his humanity; all of this is accomplished by his suffering in the flesh. When a woman whose son had been killed in a world war was told to remember how God lost his only begotten Son she replied, "He got his back." And indeed he did, in impassibility and subtlety and clarity and agility, in short in glory; but not without the omniscient Father's knowledge of a death more vicious than any known before. By being divine as well as human, Christ does not die less than us; he dies more than us, just as he thirsts more than us and hungers more than us. After all, this is the cause of his having water to quench all thirst, and bread for thousands from a few loaves, and a resurrection where once at most there had been resuscitations. We may be sealed for death from the day of our birth; the Lamb "was destined before the foundation of the world . . . " (1 Pet 1:20).

A Matter of Life and Death

Criminals are executed as a matter of justice, and the unjust die. In the case of Christ, the execution was criminal, and the just died. Of course this was to the shame of the municipality and the legal system, but it was part of a divine justice all the same: creatures cannot make amends

with their Creator, because their crime is the introduction
of death into the world, and no creature can die enough to
atone for that. Criminals pay with their own lives for
other lives, but the payment of any mortal is inadequate
satisfaction for the ruin of immortality. "Or what shall a
man give in return for his life?" (Mt 16:26). It is one thing
to kill another life, it is another thing to kill the possibility
of life. In that crime the entire human race is implicated, as
its perpetrators by the fact of being, "carrying it about",
and as its victims by having it carried out on us; this is the
terrible and splendid doctrine of original sin, which at the
same time hooks us and gets us off the hook. It was Adam's
fault, after all; but we are Adam. In Adam *all* die (I Cor.
15:22). The divine justice then proposes that death itself be
destroyed by the voluntary death of Life himself. The
injection of Life into time and space is also, then, an
inoculation against the powers of death. "The last enemy
to be destroyed is death" (I Cor 15:26). And as with any
inoculation, the procedure involves contact with the disease,
but in a body that is not yet diseased: "You know that you
were ransomed from the futile ways inherited from your
fathers, not with perishable things such as silver or gold,
but with the precious blood of Christ, like that of a lamb
without blemish or spot" (I Pet 1:18–19).

In the plainest terms, mortals cannot die enough to cancel
death. One of the severest of the early mistakes about
Christ, Monophysitism, missed this whole point in its
pious-sounding insistence that the efficacy of Christ's Passion lay in his freedom from death: he had no human nature,
and the crucifixion itself simulated death. Quite big in the
fifth century, because it sounded more "religious" than
orthodox Christianity, it keeps cropping up for the same
reason: you may find it in modernized churches where

they have replaced the crucifix with a more "resurrection-oriented" corpus usually in the form of a rather willowy figure almost ready to fly off the cross and stopped only by glue instead of nails. All playacting this, and a bad play too; it plays well in a suburban culture whose marketplaces are insulated malls and whose bravest art is automated contentment and whose corpses look healthier than when they were alive, but it is not the drama of living and dying. "Since therefore the children share in flesh and blood, he himself likewise partook of the same nature, that through death he might destroy him who has the power of death, that is, the devil, and deliver all those who through fear of death were subject to lifelong bondage. For surely it is not with angels that he is concerned but with the descendents of Abraham" (Heb 2:14–16).

Now, by virtue of his divinity Christ was free from having to die, but by virtue of that same divinity he freely chose to die "more" than any mortal can die. And to press the point, if you will, he did it in the full blush of his human liveliness, to compound the affront; he does it on a cross and not in a nursing home. Never was the wood of a cross so wooden or the blood of a body so bloody. Christ dies "more" than we can: there is more in him to die. Nothing has already died in him by sin before death. No pride has killed his love for the beauty of uncreated being. No greed has killed his love for the beauty of created being. No lust has killed his love for the beauty of love itself.

Mortal beings, having experience of sin, approach their own reflection with caution and gradually with dismay, and the older they become the more they may claim that something is wrong with the mirror or that the light is harsh. The presence of God's grace bestows a different understanding of the flesh, and ushers in with the light of each new day an intimation of age growing younger in love as it grows older in age. As that one fine old lady remarked to no one in particular after gazing at the mirror her nurse had given her: "Isn't it amazing how anyone so old can be so beautiful?" It is amazing, and it is not impossible. Youth is beautiful by nature; age is beautiful by grace. Only the good die young, they say, and that is true; but the good die young at any age. The one fountain of youth, flowing in history as a function of justice and not in fancy as a form of wishful thinking, is baptism, and where fantasy washes away decay this washes away the death behind the decay: " . . . if we walk in the light, as he is in the light, we have fellowship with one another, and the blood of Jesus his Son cleanses us from all sin. If we saw we have no sins, we deceive ourselves, and the truth is not in us. If we confess our sins, he is faithful and just, and will forgive our sins and cleanse us from all unrighteousness" (1 Jn 1:7-10).

The Last Age

We are older than we think we are, because our parents were in Paradise so long ago. Some notorious disposition of the ego wants to disregard that as some legend. There still are some charts extant from Caroline times, showing the family trees of certain peers right back to Adam and Eve, inevitably only in collateral descent from Cain. Where charts fail, hearing obtains, and the memory of the first men is heard when we hear the creak of bones as they first heard it when they passed through the tamed green of their garden to the wilds without. No such sound comes from the cross, though many other cries are there: he is as young as the world's first morning though he bears the oldest of burdens, original as sin itself, and even when the world wants to impose the creaking of decay on him some hand stays it:

> So the soldiers came and broke the legs of the first, and of the other who had been crucified with him, but when they came to Jesus and saw that he was already dead, they did not break his legs. But one of the soldiers pierced his side with a spear, and at once there came out blood and water. He who saw it has born witness—his testimony is true, and he knows that he tells the truth— that you also may believe. For these things took place that the scripture might be fulfilled, "Not a bone of him shall be broken." And again another scripture says, "They shall look on him whom they have pierced" (Jn 19:32–37).

The writers for this drama have been the prophets and God himself, from a peculiar recipe item given in Egypt to an oracle at the end of another exile, and it is no mean play. How says the other play? Six ages have passed and Shakespeare's foil has another and a last:

> Last scene of all,
> That ends this strange eventful history,
> Is second childishness, and mere oblivion;
> Sans teeth, sans eyes, sans taste, sans everything.

But what Jaques offers is too dreary for anyone alive, and some rejoinder is needed. Even if they have no image of Christ's timeless life hung on the cross, those who are feasting in the charm and shine of the dappled trees in Arden call his bluff, and along with them the character Amiens:

Blow, blow, thou winter wind
   Thou art not so unkind
      As man's ingratitude;
   Thy tooth is not so keen,
   Because thou art not seen,
      Although thy breath be rude.
Heigh, ho! sing, heigh ho! unto the green holly:
Most friendship is feigning, most loving mere folly.
    Then, heigh ho! the holly!
    This life is most jolly.

There have been more substantial protests of life and moral balance than this little song coughed up out of somewhat nervous obligation to common sense, but it is all that one man can offer on the spot of a gentle if not deeply lived life. And so we have it. Heigh ho. The bravado of a hero who does not want to die in a world of a thousand excuses to avoid death. Jesus in Jerusalem has one reason to confront death: the redemption of the human race. He cries out a seventh and last time, beyond the antiquity of earth and the old age of man, calling to the one to whom he made his first appeal: "Father, into thy hands I commend my spirit!" He cried out "with a loud voice" (Lk 23:46; cf. Mt 27:50; Mk 15:37). *"Kraxas",* says Matthew: a great cry such as banged against the hills when the Jews shouted at the sight of the Ark brought from Shiloh; and when the Philistines heard it they whispered, "A God has come into the camp!" Now God himself has come into the camp, and he cries a shout no other can make.

So he dies, and that is supposed to mean oblivion. Sans teeth, sans eyes, sans taste, sans everything. The horrid pattern is universal, and the women were set on anointing what remained and staving off the rot for at least a few days. So the drama is supposed to end, as it has for everyone and every empire since first there were such things "The tumult and the shouting dies; the captains and the kings depart . . . " But . . . if the play is over, why is the curtain not closing and why are not the house lights going on for some universal exit? "And behold, the curtain of the temple was torn in two, from top to bottom . . . " (Mt 27:51). This is Christ's drama, and when he dies the curtain opens and the lights darken because all else has been prelude and now is the beginning. The curtain torn open was the veil on the inner sanctuary of the temple; the Holy Spirit has written a play within the play, and the true sanctuary is Christ himself: " . . . we have confidence to enter the sanctuary by the blood of Jesus, by the new and living way which he opened for us through the curtain, that is, through his flesh . . . " (Heb 10:19–20).

And what then of oblivion? In a few days his teeth will bite into a piece of broiled fish, and his eyes will gaze at his astonished men as he tastes it. Then on a long familiar shore he will reach out a scarred hand and take Peter aside for words he confides to us:

> Truly, truly, I say to you, when you were young, you girded yourself and walked where you would; but when you are old, you will stretch out your hands, and another will gird you and carry you where you do not wish to go. . . . Follow me (Jn 21:18).

You and I and the world of humanity are now invited to enter his drama and make it our own as he has so long made our little acts and ages his: "Follow me."